STUDY

IN

PERFECT

ASSOCIATION

OF

WRITERS

AND

WRITING

PROGRAMS

AWARD

FOR

CREATIVE

NONFICTION

STUDY IN
PER*f*ECT

ESSAYS BY

Sarah Gorham

THE UNIVERSITY OF
GEORGIA PRESS

Athens & London

© 2014 by the University of Georgia Press
Athens, Georgia 30602
www.ugapress.org
All rights reserved
Designed by Kaelin Chappell Broaddus
Set in 9.7/14 Bodoni Twelve ITC Book
by Kaelin Chappell Broaddus
Manufactured by Thomson Shore
The paper in this book meets the guidelines for permanence
and durability of the Committee on Production Guidelines for
Book Longevity of the Council on Library Resources.

Printed in the United States of America
14 15 16 17 18 c 5 4 3 2 1

Library of Congress Cataloging-in-Publication Data
Gorham, Sarah, 1954–
Study in perfect : essays / by Sarah Gorham.
pages cm. –
(Association of writers and writing programs award for creative nonfiction)
Includes bibliographical references.
ISBN 978-0-8203-4712-7 (hardcover : alk. paper) –
ISBN 0-8203-4712-4 (hardcover : alk. paper)
I. Title.
PS3557.07554S88   2014
814'.54–dc23
2014002325

British Library Cataloging-in-Publication Data available

To Lucille,

Josephine,

Anabel Mae,

and Seamus

CONTENTS

~

ACKNOWLEDGMENTS

AGNI:	"Darling Amanita," "On Selfishness"
Alimentum:	"Sentimental à la Carte"
Arts and Letters:	"Neriage, or What Is the Secret of a Long Marriage?"
Creative Nonfiction:	"Study in Perfect," published here as "Perfect Word," "Perfect Flower," "Perfect Water," "Perfect Solution," "Perfect Tea," "Perfect Conversation," "Perfect Sleep," "Perfect Barn," "Perfect Heaven," and "Perfect Ending"
Fourth Genre:	"Marking Time in Door County"
Gulf Coast:	"The Shape of Fear"
Iowa Review:	"Moving Horizontal"
Pleiades:	"Be There No Human Here," "A Drinker's Guide to *The Cat in the Hat*"

Prairie Schooner: "Woman Drawn Twice"

Quarterly West: "On Lying"

Real Simple: "The Changeling"

Endless thanks and love to Jeffrey, my forever man.

STUDY

IN

PERFECT

INTRODUCTION

◡

The Ohio is rising. We drive down the road two or three times a day to gape at the river's ascent over docks and decks, graveled shoulders and steamy blacktop. We marvel at the water's subversion, snubbing boundaries, finding its way inside things it's not supposed to touch, like electrical boxes and river-park restrooms. It creeps into our basements and ruins immaculate lawns, a real life, mocha-colored version of the Blob. In its relentless, steady progress and its egalitarian destructiveness, it is perfect.

What can the city possibly do to stay this roiling mix of snow-melt, runoff, and rain? The sandbag is a laughable defense, like a chrysanthemum planted in a rifle's barrel (you know the photograph). Forget your well-laid escape plans and army engineer pilings. A flood's rushing water levitates picnic tables and boats like rubber bath toys. It douses everything in silt, including meticulous shrubs and mulch laid down by Operation Brightside volunteers. All their work, wiped out. Even the silvery boat barn moans as it tears from its foundation and pulls away.

So we wait till the river relents, sinks back into its rumpled bed. *Après le déluge*, the state releases emergency funds for the cleanup. Workers appear in orange vests to remake what was recently a perfectly beautiful place.

But *perfect* is a slippery term. For a word that seemingly requires no modification, it certainly has had more than its share of cultural shading. To the ancient Greeks, perfection was a requisite for beauty. The Pythagoreans specified right proportions and a harmonious arrangement of parts in their idea of perfection. To the Japanese, an object of supreme beauty must contain an *imperfection*. In his essay "Of Beauty," Sir Francis Bacon famously noted: "There is no excellent beauty that hath not some strangeness in the proportion." Immanuel Kant felt that beauty was something distinct from perfection, because it was an aesthetic question of taste. Aristotle offered the earliest and perhaps best description in three hues: Perfection is (a) that which is so good that nothing of the kind could be better; (b) that which has attained its purpose, like perfect vision or a watch that keeps perfect time; and (c) that which is complete—containing all the requisite parts. To Empedocles however, perfection depended on *incompleteness*, the potential for development and for adding new characteristics.

This book is an exploration of the many-faceted concept of perfection, which by its nature embraces imperfection. The essays alternate between brief considerations, such as "Perfect Solution" and "Perfect Heaven," and longer pieces, such as "On Lying" and "On Selfishness." In "Moving Horizontal" a Victorian house loses its charm over time, especially when compared with a modernist contemporary filled with light. The poisonous mushrooms in "Darling Amanita" lead to thoughts about our darker impulses, like obsessive love, even murder. Family life is dense with pleasure, as in the perfect vacation described in "Marking Time in Door County" and in "Neriage, or What Is the Secret of a Long Marriage?" where an ancient Japanese ceramic technique has much in common with shaping a close relationship. But there is pain too: "The Shape of Fear" relates the story of a child stricken with a deadly Staph infection; the essay reflects on the function and form of fear. Alcoholism, a family disease no one wants to talk about, is poised against *The Cat in the Hat*, a story everyone has read and enjoyed. There is such a thing as a perfect cup of tea, depending on who is preparing and drinking it ("Perfect Tea"). And schmaltzy show tunes flowing from a black-lacquered piano in a Chinese restaurant can be genuinely moving ("Sentimental à la Carte").

Thus the collection winds its way around and through the many permutations of this most hermetic and exalted concept. The book proceeds with the full consciousness that perfection's exact definition is subjective, reliant on who is speaking, and easily unmoored by time, wind, and water.

Moving Horizontal

Once, we lived our lives vertically at 1637 Rosewood, a four-over-four Victorian with finished attic. It was, we believed, the perfect house, holding most of a twenty-five-year marriage and all but three years of our two daughters' lives. Within its walls, we lived through elementary, middle, and high school, and college applications; a twenty-two-inch snowfall, a burst appendix, the euthanasia of a beloved rabbit named Meatloaf, a tornado, bunk beds, My Little Pony, multiple piercings; piano flute voice mandolin drama soccer lessons; one recovery from alcoholism and another from MRSA; Smashing Pumpkins, Modest Mouse, straight As and the first D, new drivers and five minor accidents, Nintendo arguments, a plague of mice, eighteen tall and skinny Christmas trees to fit in our foyer.

The feeling was one of containment. We were eggs in a three-story egg carton. One child lived in the attic, another in a second-floor bedroom: daughter cubicles. My husband and I slept just next door, our studies right on top of each other. Far below were the living/family/dining rooms, where everyone tossed and tumbled together. The children kept us microscopically focused with their various crises, sorrows, pleasures, and accomplishments. We were living in the "now," not mystically, but perforce. A life was *one day*, with various components, compliments, or complaints, and little thought of yesterday or tomorrow.

Two pencil-scratched growth charts on a closet door documented our daughters' progress up and out of the house. At five foot seven and five foot three, they were gone, living in tiny houses of their own in a blue-collar area of town with train tracks and a funky grocery store.

We took a deep breath and looked around.

All around us in our visual field is a world we understand and simultaneously take for granted. We assume that trees remain as they are . . . rooted in the ground. Intuitively, we understand that water seeks the low point and then seeks its level. These are subconscious phenomena that we live with every day. Most of the time I don't even like to think of what I do as "design"—as it conjures in the mind something graphic or sculptural or high-tech. I think of my process as making conceptual connections. In this case, finding things we recognize and bringing them forward, or raising them up into our field of vision.

—MICHAEL BARRY, ARCHITECT

What do you do when your house turns against you? When maintenance of the body occupies an hour of each day, with brushes and paste and tweezers and emery boards? There's the little click inside your shoulder when you do your sit-ups, and the floor responds when you lie back against it. You know the spot, where the joinery rubs and the nail squeaks.

With the children gone, we expected a sudden influx of oxygen, a second honeymoon, this one lasting a couple of decades. But the press of middle age was upon us. My father-in-law suffered a stroke, triple bypass, lung cancer, and finally died, a thin contrail of the FBI strongman he once was. The girls entered their bumpy twenties with minimum-wage jobs, romances, unsympathetic landlords—a long way yet from self-sufficiency. Indeed, with larger pressures from both younger and older generations, we felt vacuum packed. The once brand-new renovation at 1637 Rosewood, too, was not just twenty years older; it had landed in that unfashionable place between antique and contemporary, retro and old fashioned, like waist-high underpants or an AMC Gremlin or a middle-aged man who refuses to give up smoking dope.

A house is a body. Just look at the argot: dental molding, eyebrow window, face board, face brick, footer, footing, head, knee walls, nosing, shakes, sleeper, toenail. Thus, a leak in the roof is unsettling because it's like torn skin, a scorched chimney like a dirty neck. Sometimes you can waylay disgust by choosing what to see and what not to see. Don't look in the mirror. Throw away that bathroom scale. Or develop immunity, called "growing used to."

One day I let my guard down. It was midwinter. Without the healthy distraction of sunlight, I was more than a little depressed. I opened our back gate, which sat on an alley lined with trash bins and recycling containers. Next to our silver maple a half-full beer bottle, left by a homeless man who made a recessed area behind our fence his bedroom. Then, to my dismay—a spray of aqua-colored safety glass, sour cream containers, and a dozen soggy French fries, like the debris of last night's raucous party. I began to sweep in a cloud of gray dust and glass shards, pushing the mess farther into the alley, where it became the city's responsibility. My sneakers were coated with grit, as I knew my lungs were. For eighteen years, we had passed this kind of scene without seeing it.

~~~

The second thought was simply—how best to do this? The lot, as it was, being very narrow and deep, provided the answer. So long as one follows one's own line of consciousness (analytical and intuitive) about sense of place, I believe one will always find the answer.

—MICHAEL BARRY

To cheer ourselves up, we bought a shiny red Vespa, and when that was stolen, replaced it with a silver one. We buzzed down to the coffee shop, took long loops through Olmsted's Cherokee Park, unembarrassed though we knew we resembled Mama and Papa bears on a tricycle. We rode farther out of town to a scenic byway known as River Road. The air pummeled our faces; we sailed through walls of scent—sweet, damp, pine, or possum decaying. To the left, the swollen river and a barge pushing by. To the right, a lone real estate sign marked "Exquisite!" in bright yellow. A long gravel driveway extended back from the road between crumbling posts. We said *why not, let's look, we can't, oh come on, useless, no one's around, couldn't hurt, why not, OK.*

For over two centuries, Kentucky has offered up more than its share of vices, featuring a wicked blend of liquor, tobacco, and horse betting. The state produces almost all the world's bourbon and 37 percent of U.S. horse sales. Just minutes outside Louisville, the landscape dips and gently rises and horse fences painted rich brown follow suit; the animals graze in fields or bunch together under a tree, tails swatting flies. Alongside bluegrass, acres of burley tobacco flutter and the barns where the crop is air-cured rise in regular intervals. These are beautiful structures, with silvery tin roofs and charcoal-blue siding. Often the fencing is whitewashed, and in sunlight or gloom the palette is always startling and elegant. Tobacco barns inspired architect Michael Barry, who took on the task of renovating and expanding a dowdy seventies house off River Road. Its siding is now the same blue-black, the roof metallic bright, and the doors are framed in a warm, orange-tinged oak the color of dried tobacco.

We slid off the scooter, treading carefully, as if trespassing in more ways than one: the property belonged to someone else; it was likely way beyond our means, though a number of modest homes lined River Road; and finally, we had no business considering a move with one child still in college. From the front, the place was modest, a cross between a Cape Cod and a windowed barn, with garage and second-floor guest room connecting at a forty-five-degree angle. We stole around to the backyard, a large expanse of grass dropping to a creek and woods beyond. Turning around, we faced the house the way it was meant to be seen, panoramically: angled roofline to the left, a vast stretch of windows and two sets of double glass doors across the middle, punctuated by a pagodalike porch with white crossbeams and five, count them, *five* huge decks extending into the grass like a great stair. "Oh, my God," we said. We peered through the windows into the great room, where blond hardwood extended more than forty feet west, disappearing right and left into channels formed by half-walls and frosted glass. We could see a sleek cement and steel fireplace, its mantle raw cherry, the firebox set slightly off center, and could it be, there was an outdoor shower too! To call the plan "open" was an understatement; but somehow, the house was both spacious and deeply human in scale. We backed off with an "oh well," confident the price would be over a million. Heading out of the driveway, we grabbed the info sheet, which announced in bold, "You'll feel like you're on vacation!" Underneath, an asking price of less than a third of our expectation. "We could do this," we whispered simultaneously, then called our realtor, the listing agent, and both of our daughters, who all drove out to meet us. Four hours later, our bid was accepted.

As one stands in the grain of the site, facing its depth of field, one also stands in the grain of the dwelling. As few doors as possible, consciously eroded parallel walls, a kind of "sheared space," with beams extending from inside to outside—all reinforce this "in-the-grain" attitude.

—MICHAEL BARRY

Our old house had many doors—twenty-five to be exact. Pocket, closet, French, doors marked "DO NOT ENTER" covered with hex signs and skateboard logos. Behind them, the girls entered puberty, tried their first cigarettes and beer, my husband and I had covert sex and hasty arguments. We all had our secrets and, in theory, we were safe. The house was rocked by all kinds of weather, but the weather that affected us most was interior.

The new house has only *two* inside doors, both leading to lavatories. The first-floor master bedroom flows around a partition into the great room. The great room veers into the master bath, sink, and shower. The kitchen pours into the great room. Large open "windows" front the guest bedroom, though there is no glass, only space, and a discrete stairway rises from the foyer.

We could bowl in this place, or contra dance with a dozen couples. We could throw a wedding, or hold an auction, or hire a Big Band orchestra. We could run laps, ice skate, shot-put; the possibilities were endless. We stretched out on the taut, bare floor and let the dogs flop and sniff.

No whining or squeaking or inch-long splinters; no creases, dents, or sun damage; no history at all. The house gave us a new skin and permission to explore it. The house was young, unembarrassed in its nudity, and so were we. This was *horizontal* living, our past and future laid out at once, in the open, where we could see it. Which doesn't mean we were untouched by difficulty; we just had the sudden oxygen and range to consider it all.

I grew up with a deep respect for all things antique, objects that survived fashion, sturdy enough to last hundreds of years. My grandmother gifted me a set of flow-blue dishes from the 1800s, a French writing desk from the 1700s, nine miniature portraits with piano-key frames. I tried to avoid stores like IKEA selling trendy furniture that would most likely be dust in a decade. We were both raised on the East Coast and our furniture fit well in the Rosewood place with its early 1900s atmosphere of compressed history and withheld energy. Shaker chairs with sagging cane seats, rabbit holes inside a cupboard– these objects contained centuries.

In the new house, so tuned to the sprawling Kentucky landscape, they looked fussy and stubborn–in short, ridiculous. We used the fireplace as an anchor, threw down a small rug, shuffled the couch, captain's chairs, and recliners around it. Seating for six, theoretically. But in a forty-foot great room, the rug felt like a raft, chairs and couch legs hanging on like shipwreck survivors. The floorboards established an east/west current, better left unimpeded–no dams or backsplashes. Without banisters, balustrades, carpeting, doors, partitions, or skid tape to keep from slipping, we slipped. The dogs spun around corners, back legs flying. At first we were disoriented, confused. How to settle, where to step first? Should we bother with furniture at all or just throw down a few sleeping bags?

For more than fifty years, every step we've taken has been shadowed by 78 million fellow baby boomers. We were born in a crowd, schooled, worked, married, divorced, remarried, had 1.86 children. Now little explosions are going off everywhere as boomers empty their kids' bedrooms, enjoy a little free time, and maybe even some discretionary income. You can track our interests by watching the Food Network or HGTV or a flock of tourists visiting vineyards. On a whim, my friends Leslie and Bill purchased land in Costa Rica and plan to spend half the year there. Stephen divorced, remarried an intelligent, gorgeous woman and finds himself a father again at fifty-five. His last email, written in a sleepless fog, announced they were calling the child Elvis. We'll retire in a crowd and die in a crowd. When we get to that point, there'll be a national ad campaign for ashes shot into space or your DNA mapped and published. It'll happen. We're already seeing "green" cemeteries, where biodegradable caskets or burial shrouds of natural fibers are used, and graves are placed randomly throughout a woodland or meadow, marked with the planting of a tree or shrub.

––––––

The new house opened our eyes to design and, like thousands of others, we surfed the Internet for knockoff Sapien tower bookcases that would put our books within reach but not clutter the landscape of our great room. We shifted a small vase on the mantle until, slightly off center, it looked exactly right. On our backyard deck, we placed five Ronde armchairs, all facing southeast, like seagulls headfirst into the wind. Not coincidentally, our mailbox was stuffed with catalogs from CB2 and West Elm, and we understood the slick TV ad in which a black-suited woman sits before her condescending architect, pulls a Kohler faucet from her purse, and says, "Design a house around *this*."

The door is a missing piece of wall; sometimes a wall is closed and sometimes the wall is open.
—MICHAEL BARRY

Even where walls were necessary, Michael minimized their effect by cutouts, half-walls, artful absences, and subtle irregularity. A larger symmetry was implied, not doggedly spelled out. Wherever possible, he dispensed with traditional trim. Instead, between sheetrock and frame, he built a half-inch indentation, like an irrigation channel. It adds an elegance and depth to the joinery. It seems more truthful to the juxtaposition of two dissimilar materials, this crevice of shadow and mystery—a mixing space, as well as a little breathing room. We run our fingers inside when turning a corner, like caressing the valleys between knuckles.

Side by side at the dinner table, my husband and I chew silently, each of us absorbed in a book. We work in separate wings of the house, but this distance can be intimate too. Across the great room, he shouts, "Can you get the phone? Please?" Or: "Do you have a minute? I want to read you something." Sometimes we have no choice but to listen to each other. Sneezes, snores, sighs, the rattle of keypads, the dog on the couch licking a ripe spot–sound leaves its source, gullies, ambles, spreads. There's a strange noise somewhere and, like ship radar, we rotate our heads about, trying to locate it.

In a vertical dwelling, we stand at attention, prepared for battle, whether the conflict simmers in adolescence or the obstinacy of aged parents. We are backbones when their own skeletons are evolving or devolving. We are fence posts, traffic signs, door frames. We mark their territory and ours–this is where you should go, this not. I was always on my feet in the old house, which also was on its feet, and had been for more than a hundred years.

Now in middle age, our vision's softer, taste buds not so discerning, and one ear catches only a half-conversation at best. We've been knocked about enough to learn that no plan is a sure thing, no matter how well structured, and no body will last, no matter how well maintained. Our new house celebrates the gray areas, dissolves categories, subverts traditional outlines. A vertical house, with its right and proper posture, holds. A horizontal house releases.

Shortly after we moved in, we discovered we weren't the first to take residence since the sale. Twenty feet down the chimney, just above the flue, was a nest of barn swallows. Outside

I watched the female swoop from sky to nest without pausing to readjust her aim. Then the thrumming of her young began, faint at first, but as the summer wore on, nearly deafening, primordial. We could hardly talk without acknowledging the famished creatures. They outgrew the nest, three of them bouncing into our living room, slamming into the windows, frantic, till we could chase them down with a thrown dishtowel. Here and there, droppings on sills, stretchers, beams—evidence of their panic. My husband bought a wire screen for the chimney, but we never got around to mounting it. We were human, after all, and rather liked the role we played in nature—this swallow drama. A small part, but essential: cupping the fledglings in terrycloth, we carried them gingerly to the porch.

The birds did the rest.

PER *f* ECT
Word

Serendipity, tasty to look at, a bright experiment for the mouth. Leading off, the meditative hum, *seren*, like a flat horizon. Then the playful up and down of the last three syllables as if our boat has encountered chop.

She flipped off the trampoline, knocking over the soldier who would soon become her lover. Isaac Newton was not beaned by a falling apple, but it's a more perfect truth, the one we love and remember. A moon called Charon emerged from a "defect" in a photograph. Before departing for vacation, Alexander Fleming failed to disinfect his bacteria cultures, only to find them contaminated with *Penicillium* when he returned.

Thoreau said, "There is a certain perfection in accident which we never consciously attain."

There is also a certain accident in perfection, which favors the prepared mind.

Darling Amanita

Noli me tangere. (Touch me not.)

Halfway through Bo Widerberg's 1967 film *Elvira Madigan*, the camera pans over a summer pasture with trees encircling. The sun is resplendent, and soon blond Elvira in her long striped skirt and white peasant blouse stumbles out of the woods with her paramour, a handsome soldier from the Swedish Army. The story is true: Thirty-four-year-old Lieutenant Count Bengt Edvard Sixten Sparre abandoned his post and family for the twenty-one-year-old acrobatic dancer, whose parents ran a small circus. Sixten and Elvira fled to the island of Tåsinge in Denmark, where they lived for barely two weeks.

In the film, the couple is starving, famished, and falls upon a scattering of mushrooms. They drop to their knees and stuff the mushrooms wildly into their mouths without washing or chewing. Later they are sick like animals in high grass. Perhaps *Amanita fulva*, or tawny grisette, was the culprit. This species is found in conifer, birch, beech, and oak woodlands in Europe, and, like most amanitas, it causes vomiting, gastrointestinal distress, and sometimes death. But the mushrooms don't kill Elvira and her lover. After thirteen days, Sixten knows their situation is hopeless and walks to town, where he spends the small remainder of their money on wine, bread, olives, fruit, herring–a lavish picnic lunch. They meander into a nearby forest, the Nørreskov, and make love one last time. Sparre draws his service revolver, shoots Elvira, and then himself.

It's tragic, but not unheard of–even the most transcendent romance can double as a kind of poison, leading us to abandon our senses, families, careers, health, and sometimes, our lives.

We recognize two types of mushroom washers: those who scrub (with water), those who wipe (with towels). The first care not for the mushroom's integrity, only that it is clean, absolutely clean. A cotton dishtowel is spread next to the sink, the cold-water tap runs full blast. In her hand the scrubber holds a wooden mushroom brush with soft bristles, but as she plucks the mushrooms one by one from their blue cardboard box, she is not gentle. Every spot, every flake of peat is obliterated, till the mushroom, which absorbs water like a sponge, is exhausted and lies sodden on the towel. Sauté them and diners will be safe, but the mushroom turns soupy, is no longer firm to the bite.

The second have seen the mushroom videos. A hangar-like cool space, or a cave. Tables layered with humus, stretching far as the eye can see. The "wiper" is less fearful of bacteria, convinced by these documentarylike images. No one has studied the long-term health effects of mushroom washing. Has anyone died, by either method? Suffered nausea or parasites? Holding the mushroom by the stem, she brushes off the soil with a chamois or paper towel, careful to preserve the cap's virgin condition. A wiper relishes the spring of its flesh against her knife. The mushroom is composed almost entirely of water, quite a trick, so why swamp its accomplishment?

In matters of love and dining, we are adventurous. Or not.

Once there was a naturalist named L. John Trott, who taught eighth grade at a small private school in Virginia. The L stood for "Little," to distinguish him from his father, John Trott. An unfortunate coincidence, as in fact he stopped growing at only five foot two. His science curriculum consisted of ornithology and botany, with a little textbook chemistry thrown in to please the parents. Students were deeply engaged in bird banding, plant identification, and the natural histories of a dozen species.

In April one year, he led his class down a woodsy trail, pausing to identify rue anemone, bloodwort, and the demure spring beauty clustered at the base of an oak. "Ah," he said, "here's something interesting, destroying angel, or *Amanita phalloides*–from the Latin *phallus*; the immature mushroom is shaped like an erect penis." (Sudden interest in shoe tips. Relief when he went on.)

"Very dangerous," he said, pulling a pair of leather gloves from his jacket, stretching them over his hands, waving his circle of fourteen-year-olds back, back, back, before he knelt. Next to the leaves, he laid a finger on each section of the mushroom, beginning with the pileus–"like an umbrella," he explained, "designed to protect the scissor-blade gills, which in turn protect the spores, microscopic 'seeds,' rather like our sperm"–(sideways glances)–"which you'll never see with the naked eye unless you make a spore print, but that's another lesson. Here then is the stipe and, ringing it, a partial veil or annulus. Most significant of all, the volva–consider the female anatomy–a semidetached cup at the base of the stem. By this you'll know amanita. But be aware, the cup is often buried beneath soil or a rock."

Sometime later, he brushed a lash from the crook of his left eye. A wayward spore burned halfway through his cornea before he arrived at the hospital.

From that point on, Little John was a changed man. His students forever associated mushrooms with cantankerous pirates, thanks to the eye patch he wore.

Amanita phalloides is an easily bruised, pale beauty, the color of milk glass in its momentary prime, mature carriage like a tiny Greek temple. One bite, and you have boarded a subway to the grave. Amatoxins are the lethal component of amanita. They resist changes in temperature and are quickly absorbed by the intestines. The estimated lethal dose is 0.1 mg/kg, or 7 mg of toxin in adults. Six to thirty-six uneventful hours may pass after ingestion. Then nausea, vomiting, diarrhea, and abdominal pain begin in earnest. After a while, there's momentary relief as symptoms subside. If you were planning to drive to the hospital, you might change your mind, assume the worst is over. This latent period is why amanita is often fatal. Quietly, with little show, amatoxins invade the liver and kidneys. Without treatment, the result is coma or death.

Seeing one, you might think pedestal, or plinth, not toadstool–the nickname, ever since the fourteenth century, for all poisonous mushrooms. The word comes from the Middle English *tadde* and *stole* and stemmed from a fear that toads themselves were deadly poison. Variations include tadstoles, frogge stoles, tadstooles, tode stoles, frogstooles, paddockstool, puddockstool, paddocstol, toadstoole, paddockstooles, and toodys hatte.

Innocent as sugar
but full of paralysis:
to eat
is to stagger down.
—MARY OLIVER

We keep our distance from catastrophe—invisible, silent, or otherwise. Our brains are hard at work on self-preservation. But powerful as our instinct is to stay alive, we also crave knowledge, excitement, and pleasure. The germ of touching begins in the brain—first as a mild curiosity, then as a spur to action.

By sight, the most omnipresent amanita is *muscaria*. Wherever the image of a mushroom is called for—in children's literature, greeting cards, kitschy seventies needlepoint—its features appear: white stem and a bright-red, umbrella-shaped cap with marked white flecks or "warts." The common name is fly agaric. In the Middle Ages crushed *muscaria* in a dish of milk attracted flies, which then grew drowsy and drowned. Even today the mushroom is used as an insecticide. It's also possible the nickname derives from the medieval belief that insanity was caused by flies invading the brain.

The agaric is considered poisonous. But in small doses it's a well-known hallucinogen. The psychoactive ingredient is muscimol, most potent in the layer of skin just below the cap. Like tryptamine (found in another hallucinogenic mushroom, *Psilocybin*), muscimol mimics the effects of serotonin on the brain. Symptoms occur thirty minutes to two hours after ingestion and include dilation of pupils, confusion, repetitive actions, euphoria, a feeling of unusual strength, distortions of body and time, and visual hallucinations.

Four-thousand-six-hundred-year-old hieroglyphs from Egypt suggest that the agaric was considered a gate to immortal life, but only royalty could indulge. Certain Vikings in Scandinavia ate the mushrooms and, in war, rampaged unmanageably; they came to be known as Berserkers, hence one likely origin of the word *berserk*. In eastern Siberia, *A. muscaria* was used recreationally as well as religiously. The Koryak tell the story of the god Vahiyinin, who spat upon the earth, and his spittle became the warty mushroom. Big Raven consumed the mushroom, which enabled him to carry a whale to its home. He was so elated with his new powers, he begged the god to scatter the agaric far and wide so that his people could experience it too. Western Siberians were less fortunate. There, only the shaman could eat the mushroom to induce a trance state; the rest of the tribe drank his urine, where the active ingredient persisted, sans toxicity.

In his book *The Greek Myths*, Robert Graves hypothesizes that the Dionysian rites were conducted under the influence of *Amanita muscaria*. Other researchers have conjectured that agaric was used by Moses, Elijah and Elisha, Isaiah, Ezekiel, Jonah, even Jesus and his disciples. A 1291 fresco in Plaincourault, France, shows the agaric right alongside Adam, Eve, the Serpent, and the Tree of Knowledge. Eve bends forward, her hand resting on her distended abdomen, perhaps in warning to potential users.

⁓

To "mushroom" is to expand rapidly. To "pop up like mushrooms" is to appear suddenly, as if overnight. In fact, all species of mushrooms take several days to form, beginning with the pin stage, followed by a button stage. Finally, the mushroom draws in water quickly and can swell to full size in a few hours. As Emily Dickinson observed, "Doth like a bubble antedate, / And like a bubble hie."

⁓

Lewis Carroll, Victorian storyteller with a questionable attraction to little girls, was a known experimenter with fly agaric. *Alice in Wonderland*'s body warps and quick travels through time were probably inspired by agaric-induced hallucinations. In one scene, Alice is instructed by a hookah-smoking caterpillar to nibble from the mushroom he sits on. She grows immense with a bite from one side, miniscule when she eats from the other. Her neck stretches grotesquely, her arms poke out of the chimney and two upstairs windows. She's able to hear animals talk, bicker, sing. A croquet ball morphs into a hedgehog, a baby into a pig.

The story of a little girl's daring and its unusual consequences impacted culture for decades to come. In the sixties,

Grace Slick's song "White Rabbit" included the infamous lyric:

> One pill makes you larger
> And one pill makes you small
> And the ones that mother gives you
> Don't do anything at all
> Go ask Alice
> When she's ten feet tall

The era brought a desire for transformation through sexual freedom, a mind-bending rock 'n' roll soundtrack, and renewed interest in magic mushrooms–chiefly *Psilocybin*, but also *Russula*, *Panaeolus*, *Stropharia*, *Boletus*, and *Amanita muscaria*. (Most hallucinogenic mushrooms are now illegal in the United States. But it's still possible to purchase the agaric on the web at just twenty-nine dollars an ounce–no stems, just caps!)

Over time the mushroom has become a symbol of metamorphosis and dark knowledge. For decades it lies low, subterranean, under the radar. Whenever a culture longs for adventure, hungers for something deeper and wilder (Lewis Carroll under the rule of Queen Victoria, Jefferson Airplane flying out of the American fifties), the mushroom rises from the loam. Its odor is musky, the scent of decay and lust.

"Had nature an Iscariot," noted Emily Dickinson, "That mushroom,–it is him." What we see on the surface–the mushroom's pileus, stipe, and gills–is the reproductive organ of an underground fungus. A network of minute threads, called hyphae, gather into a root system called the mycelium, which can be tiny, too small to see, or massive. Mycelium is crucial in ecosystems on land and in water. It decomposes plant material and, in the process, releases carbon dioxide back into the atmosphere. It enables plants to absorb water and protects against diseases. Some say the largest organism in the world is a contiguous growth of mycelium in eastern Oregon, estimated to be more than 1,665 football fields in size. A mycelium can live for years, centuries even, waiting for the right moment, the perfect mix of temperature and damp, to cast forth its curious, sometimes deadly fruit.

If you are walking through the woods, your gaze fixated on the treetops, and by accident crush a cluster of mushrooms below, never fear that in your clumsiness you have destroyed the last remaining *Russula silvicola*, *Boletus aereus*, or *Amanita citrina*. More likely, you've spread the spores more widely than the mushroom could have by itself.

"Our kind multiplies," wrote Sylvia Plath in her poem "Mushrooms." "We shall by morning / Inherit the earth. / Our foot's in the door."

The apple is a sweet-smelling fruit with the pleasing shape of a sphere—a spiritual whole, emblem of completeness. Its domain is above ground, saturated with sunshine and fresh air. When Adam and Eve desired God's knowledge, they plucked the apple from the Tree of Life and were separated from the Peaceable Kingdom forever.

The mushroom is far less exalted, rooted in the underworld, dirty. Its odor is dank and rotten. But, driven by the darker of

Freud's two energies–named for Thanatos, god of dissolution, negation, destruction, and death–we stoop and pick it up.

If we consume a magic mushroom while we are uneasy, depressed, or in some other gloomy emotional state, the experience can backfire. Once in a while, a mentally unstable user might suffer post-traumatic stress disorder or long-term hallucinatory flashbacks. Centuries ago, the Roman emperor Nero declared *Amanita muscaria* "the food of the gods" because it offered passage to a paradise from which the mushroom eater could return. But his rule (and that of many other emperors) was marked by decadence and sexual debauchery–a slouching toward the eventual fall of the empire. Legendary fatalities from mushrooms abound; the Buddha, for example, or the Holy Roman Emperor Charles VI, who died of amatoxin poisoning after eating a dish of what he thought were tasty sautéed mushrooms. His death led to the War of Austrian Succession. Said Voltaire, "This dish of mushrooms changed the destiny of Europe."

Like any action with an equal and opposite reaction, temptation has its consequences. Perhaps the apple and mushroom aren't really that far apart; they both promise godlike, forbidden knowledge. And they both come with a caveat: possible death. The mystery comes in our knowing the odds and choosing to taste anyway. We are the only animal whose imagination encompasses both transcendence and death. Yet we go for it. We taste.

Early Danish records raise the possibility that Elvira never saw what was coming. She was discovered in a position that suggested she was shot while sleeping, and her sisters claimed Elvira was a practical person, more interested in fleeing circus life than in falling so devastatingly in love. Quite simply, she saw Sixten as her passage out. To those who knew him well, the dashing lieutenant was far from the romantic hero exemplar. He was cynical, wasteful, a man with a serious gambling problem.

Despite all this, the doomed couple entered romantic mythology forever. The legend of two attractive young people who abandon social responsibility, defy moral convention, and finally die, all for illicit love, proved irresistible. We want to remember their story as Dickinson recalled her duplicitous mushroom: "The surreptitious scion / Of summer's circumspect." Perhaps we've stepped over some threshold of risk ourselves, bending to touch something taboo, intoxicating, lethal. Or if conscience and better sense prevailed, we at least want to read about it, listen, watch, and whisper the story to each other, not necessarily in warning, but in forbidden pleasure.

The tale of Elvira and Sixten became a ballad, composed by Johan Lindström Saxon. The couple was buried together in 1889, in an unmarked grave in the Landet churchyard in Tåsinge. When Bo Widerberg's film made them famous, a small marker was installed where, according to custom, new brides place flowers for the wedding bouquet that Elvira never received. It's a lush, photogenic spot lined with small pebbles, lots of shade, and gray-green lichens. When the rains come and conditions are just right, perhaps an amanita will surface—ghost in a veil, destroying angel, "its whole career," as Dickinson observed, "shorter than a snake's delay."

Flower

Having both stamens and carpels,
present and functional.

I saw a photograph of the pregnant man. He'd (she'd) under-
gone testosterone treatments, shaved off his long black hair,
grown a sketchy mustache and beard, but somehow left his
(her) uterus intact. He and his female partner appeared on
Oprah and in the pages of *People* magazine. Their child was
due in a few months, though the couple would not be feeding
the baby in the natural way. The photo clearly revealed a pair of
lateral sickle-moon scars where his breasts had been surgically
removed. Transgender groups everywhere were not pleased,
said the public was not prepared for so radical a sight. There
would be a casting of stones, and who knows what else.

A perfect flower in botanical terms is bisexual, a hermaphro-
dite. The female sexual parts include eggs, ovary, and style.
Most resemble a suction bulb, with large swelling at the base,
a stalk, and a froth of pollen-hungry styles at the tip. The male

parts look like tiny reflex hammers and consist of anther (tip) and filament (stalk). A lily in the wild is an ideal, a beautifully structured thing, even more so when viewed under a magnifying glass.

The man is to flower as gossip is to teach.

The Changeling

Beckie was born in 1960, unplanned, the last in a string of five daughters. As an infant she was sweet, sleepy, and undemanding. The family was smitten; mother nursed, nuzzled, petted her new baby, and her sisters happily accepted a warm and pliant version of their stiff plastic dolls. At seven, I was the eldest and most eager for attention; I fought to hold her, twisting toward my father's Rolleiflex. Photographs from Beckie's early years show an adorable, fluffy-haired child, four girls bent protectively around her. The crib was pulled out of storage and reassembled, baby clothes reclaimed from the dollhouse. Plenty of love to go around.

Not until six months did our parents admit something was wrong. Baby books are filled with penciled milestones. Beckie's was virtually blank. No enchanted gaze following a red teething ring, no head held up decisively, no rolling over, no sitting, no creeping. Finally, they sought help.

Physicians at Johns Hopkins University sketched a dismal picture: The child was born microcephalic, profoundly retarded with traces of cerebral palsy. Like the bound foot of a Chinese princess, her brain was in a tiny box and could advance only so far. Developmentally, she'd never be older than ten or eleven months, if that–a baby before it learns to feed itself, walk, speak, use the toilet. They advised institutionalization. My parents shot back: *Impossible*. And so, with doctors, friends, and relatives shaking their heads in collective disbelief, we began life with our healthy-daughter-sister-imposter, our changeling.

It helped that she was sweet, with radish cheeks. Mother effortlessly lifted her from bath to changing table to crib. At three, she could have been an off-the-charts baby, big for her age–that was all. A halo of dark brown curls gave the impression her skull was normal in size, and as for her eyes, sailing about, guttering near her nose, everyone knew someone with a wandering eye. She never cried, even when we lifted her smocked sundress and found a purple knitting needle puncturing one thigh. This little girl was no mistake, no accident. She grinned easily, and the milkman, postman, and all kinds of strangers made pleasant chirping noises at the sight of her.

Tenderness and light: Mother in blue jeans and poor-boy sweater gliding between sink and high chair where Beckie gnaws her terrycloth bib. Mother chops little squares of liver sausage, Edam cheese, banana, and Cheerios on a small cutting board. In one generous motion she spreads them across the plastic tray like a salesman with his samples, and Beckie reaches, lifts them to her face, her chopstick fingers scissoring. Our Westie sits in a hopeful posture beneath her chair. He knows the routine. Next spooning the applesauce, pudding, oatmeal into her mouth, catching the half that dribbles down, then spooning again. It's a serene moment: eating is Beckie's pleasure and Beckie's eating is my mother's pleasure. We girls banter and spin happily around this quiet corona.

Touch of gloom: It's naptime, which mother will get to when she finishes the dishes. Meanwhile, Beckie sprawls diagonally on her back across the kitchen doorway. In one hand, a plastic bottle of milk, which escapes her sawing fingers and rolls away. As I step across her I notice she has stopped reaching. Her eyes are creamy white with a poppy-seed speck in the center. Something is wrong, very wrong. Her eyes have rolled back into her head. She's at the bottom of a white lake, blinking. She's *blind*. I scream for my mother, who swoops in with a rag, irritated, dabbing, tsking. "It's just milk. She missed her mouth. That's all. Now go find something to do."

If my parents felt unlucky, misunderstood, unfairly burdened, I never heard. If there was guilt or anger or desperation, all was withheld, reserved for the early morning hours when the girls were asleep in every reach of the house from attic to basement. When they awoke, the house bustled. Beckie in the high chair, Beckie on her rubber mat, the sour smell of used diapers and Desitin, which mother applied to both rear end and face. The clamor and lineup for "hair-fixing time"—five girls, two braids each. Or "stair-fixing time," when we removed the newspapers, books, toys, games, sunglasses on three flights of steps, cleared out a safe-walking zone. Or laundry—clean diapers folded into thirds stacked almost three feet high. Beckie's laundry occupying half of the couch, the remainder, everyone else's. Our parents persisted, buoyant and conscientious, chasing what they thought was best for Beckie.

In the midsixties, this meant embracing the techniques of Doman and Delacato, scientists at Johns Hopkins. Their theories were a pragmatic elaboration of a much older notion, that ontogeny (or the stages of an organism's growth) recapitulates phylogeny (the evolutionary history of a species). Crawling, creeping, crude walking, and mature walking, in that order, mirror the process of human evolution from amphibian to reptile to mammal. A mentally retarded child, they reasoned, must master this exact progression if she is to develop normally. Treatment, known as "patterning," required the patient to move repeatedly through the physical motions of each phylogenetic stage. For example, in the homolateral crawling phase, the child crawls by turning her head from side to side and extending the leg and arm of the opposite side. If she cannot do this herself, three to four adults must manipulate the movements for her. The purpose of the exercise was to impose the correct "pattern" onto the central nervous system. Doman and Delacato's claim was that mentally retarded children could improve, even progress normally, as long as the exercises were repeated for at least five minutes, four times a day.

Four times a day, volunteers from all over the neighborhood knocked at our double front door and made their way up to Beckie's room—Yenta and Gretchen from the downstairs apartment, Georgia and Nancy several blocks away. We girls filled in when there was a vacancy, and there was always a vacancy. We lifted Beckie onto a folding table and stationed ourselves: the youngest moved her head, the other two worked her limbs. And all rhythmically, as if she were a rowing machine or printing press. Yenta taught us Yugoslavian rounds and everyone sang with the forced cheer of camp counselors. Patterning punctuated our day: morning, noon, afternoon, and evening. Under my hands I felt Beckie's chapped skin, hair, thin wrists and thighs, which I noticed grew more and more muscular as the year wore on. But little else developed from our family's extraordinary effort.

————

Normal babies use Jolly Jumpers, cribs, walkers outfitted with wheels and toys, and then only briefly. But no home of a profoundly retarded child would be complete without:

The Creeping Box. Built by my father from scrap lumber and padded vinyl, with eight-inch "walls" on each side. Both ends were open and one was propped up so Beckie could use the box as a kind of chute, slide down on her belly, accelerating her creep across the floor. My little sister Jenny played there and remembers the box sensually–shiny orange fabric that clung to her skin in the heat, a secret place for Chatty Cathy and her friends.

The Helmet. Padded inside, black leather out, a pliable hard-hat designed to protect her skull. When Beckie learned to sit, legs straight out in a V, she also began to bang her forehead, bending from the waist, knocking repeatedly *thud thud thud thud* against the floorboards. No one knew why, but we'd heard even normal kids did it sometimes. We bought an extra helmet, which she dangled from one hand like a big black yoyo.

The Bed Bars. These were anchored underneath the mattress with two long stay rods, when she grew too large for a crib. One morning, we found her pulled up to a standing position in the bed, both hands wrapped around the top bar, ready to pitch forward on her face. Another time she wedged a leg underneath the lowest bar, which pinned her facedown against the mattress. My father dragged a dresser over, flush with the bed, which now resembled a fortress.

One bright afternoon, mother stood at the front door, shaking her keys. "Want to go outside? Outside?" Beckie balanced against my sister Kim, who held her lightly under one arm.

Nancy was stationed halfway to the open door. Again the steel rattle of keys, Mom's high soprano–"Outside? Outside?" In the excitement, Beckie forgot she was holding on to anyone. She flung one leg out, hauled the other along, uneven this, jerky that, right, left, like a robot on ice. Down the hall she came on her own two feet. She lurched past Nancy without even looking, then tumbled into my mother's arms. Her first, magnificent steps. She was six.

What I remember is vertigo, a sudden swooping back, as if I were perched somewhere above the crown molding. So this is what she looks like vertically. All her horizontal oddities were exaggerated, with a few new ones thrown in. Beckie like a drunk flamingo. Beckie with her hands dangling from her wrists, one elbow cocked up, the other tight against her chest. Her body was a jumble of sharp angles, the chaos before the tent poles go up.

What were we clapping for? Was something fixed? Would everything turn out all right now? My mother's face was radiant.

There are numerous, often cruel labels for someone like Beckie–backward, handicapped, mentally challenged, simpleton, imbecile, tard, freak, slowpoke. I don't remember what my parents called her, but during the sixties the PC expression was "exceptional," with its upper-crust implications. That was an *exceptional* dinner. He is an *exceptionally* handsome young man. As if we could alter the troublesome deficit by dressing it up in an evening gown.

I was an enthusiastic reader, impatient with abstraction and inaccuracy, and therefore chose to call my sister what she was– mentally retarded. Before my friends could ask, before they set foot in our front hall, I prepared them. For Checker Ives in her handmade miniskirt and fishnet stockings, for socially prominent Bridget Walker, who fell silent when she saw my sister's sloppy lips pressed up against the window, I held my hands up, one above the other, miming a diagnostic chart. "Here is a ladder with four rungs," I explained. "Mildly retarded is at the top–those kids are lucky–then moderately, severely, and last of all, profoundly. My sister can't even reach the bottom rung. She's microcephalic. IQ of about ten months." Why not admit it right away, rather than suffer their confusion and stunned embarrassment? I cultivated a circle of friends who knew my story from the inside. Birdie Mintz's brother was mildly retarded. Frances Strong's little sister had seizures. Birdie and Frances and I found each other, or we were nudged together by our parents, I don't remember.

As much as possible, I held the others at arm's length, slept over at their houses, met them in the park, or at school. Unlike my cousins, who lived three blocks away, and whose house was constantly filled with visitors, the Gorhams entertained only when we had to. Even now, I grow fidgety and tense with dinner guests around.

For a few precious years, Beckie was cute. Then she was not so cute, her body an awkward combination of rigidity and slackness. There was no hiding the diaper bulge, or the tea towel knotted around her neck. As she grew, her difference grew. She made her mark on me, like the mole on my right foot, which I tried to hide by wearing sneakers in the summer. But there was no hiding Beckie. We were connected by blood, tissue, skin. Inside her lopsided head, all through her body was genetic material I shared, like it or not.

Mother and I wheeled Beckie in her scuffed-up stroller to the park, fully aware she was strange, and that made us strange, and every eye was on us while we crossed the dusty baseball field. We headed to the tot playground, where the swings had metal bars to lock her in. The other kids were half her size, unabashed in their curiosity. I wanted to whirl the stroller about and flee home before I perished from humiliation. But Mom set a stubborn example of patience and education, answered their questions, let the little ones hold her hands, instructed them in Beckie's gentleness. It was our duty.

God was a responsible creator, or so went the theory. He permitted only those evils that encouraged goodness, which made us humane and just. Retarded children are a tragedy, but they are also the triggers for compassion, philanthropy, scientific research. Indeed, Beckie gave birth to my mother's avocation. Finding few services for the handicapped and no central source of information, my mother created Washington's first *Directory of Services for the Handicapped*. Later, she became director of the Montgomery County Association for Retarded Citizens, a job she assumed while Beckie was in "school."

Eager to please, my sisters and I joined her–educating, enlisting, converting. Dad raised up a tent on the sidewalk, and we sold lemonade for the retarded. Nancy volunteered at state institutions, reading and providing companionship to the retarded. We all sold fruitcakes for the retarded–Claxton fruitcakes in red-and-white striped boxes, three dense, ingotlike bars to a box. Every fall we sent out an appeal to friends and family, with Beckie's photograph at the top. "Dear Friends," one letter began, typed on my mother's Royal typewriter and dated November 15, 1967:

This fall Beckie was seven years old, and like all solid citizens of seven, went off to school. However, unlike most, she was found eligible for admission by only one school in the entire area. It was the Co-op School for Handicapped Children in Vienna, VA, which does *not* require that its students talk, or know what a potty is for. In short, Beckie passed its nonrequirements with flying colors. She loves her new school, and has seemed happier, more alert, and more responsive since attending its "classes" with her school-mates.

But our joy was somewhat dampened by a notice from the school informing us that in *this* Co-op, cooperating means selling unappetizing quantities of fruitcakes. And so . . . . . . you have been chosen to share our burden. Will you buy a pound or two of fruitcake? It costs $1.10 per pound. Delivery is guaranteed. It happens, by the way, to be very good fruitcake, which makes it easier for us–and you. Call us any time at FE8-1765. Our staff of assistants will be happy to take your order.

Fondly, All the Gorhams.

Dear reader, we were that staff of assistants. Our house was a processing center, with each of Beckie's sisters stamping, packaging, taping, writing out addresses, licking labels and envelopes. I can't even tell you if we liked the stuff, which crowded our freezer and grew fur by June. I will confess that I dug out the green and red cherries, leaving the rutted cake on the countertop to dry. What a team we were!

Beckie was our *wabi*, the distinctive flaw that made our family an exquisite paragon. This Japanese concept, with its sister *sabi*, guides us with three important principles: nothing lasts, nothing is finished, and nothing is perfect. Asymmetry, asperity, oddity, and incompletion have a place in art and life! Indeed, *wabi-sabi* can lead us to enlightenment. Here was something to crow about. So I crowed, reviewing books for a journal of exceptional children, writing reports on the retarded, combing through library catalogs, hungry for literature that portrayed them as human, with sisters and brothers and aunts, like us. *The Sound and the Fury, Of Mice and Men*, and especially, *To Kill a Mockingbird*. Atticus was my hero, mother and father blended into one. I loved that next-door tree with its mysterious, miraculous knothole. In the movie, their neighborhood was bathed in lustrous black and white, with wailing screen doors and wicked-witch branches. We called my sister "Boo," for the sensitive Mr. Radley who emerged from the Halloween shadows.

Then she pitched into adolescence and we had to admit her presence was not so benign. It was consuming just to maintain the all clear in our house—dishes, silverware, homework, potting soil, nail scissors, dirty socks, crayons, Coke bottles—everything went in her mouth, or crashed to the floor. Her nose was crusty, her teeth crooked and difficult to clean. Saliva soaked her T-shirts, and the collars were often ripped from ceaseless chewing. She had moments of over-the-top excitement. If an ambulance passed at full scream, Boo threw herself down on the sidewalk and flapped like a beached seal, her pleasure bodywide. At first, this was funny. Then not so funny. In the Bethesda garden center, or Kmart, or the Giant, we let her drive the cart, dragging that leg as if it were made of steel. Inevitably, something would set her off. The Muzak shifted, the intercom chimed, and down she went, fanning herself deliriously, oblivious to startled housewives and sales clerks on alert. The sight of my sister stirred something deep and disorienting in others—a baby in a teenager's body, the damaged child as monster, from the Latin *monere*, "to warn."

My parents agreed to experiment and place Boo in a "boarding school" with an excellent reputation. The results were disastrous. Staff-to-patient ratio was poor and Beckie deteriorated quickly. I accompanied my mother on her last visit through the Pennsylvania suburbs to Woods School. We were directed to a pool, where Beckie was taking swimming lessons. She sat on a bench, dwarfed in her lifejacket—a wispy, bony little bird. She'd lost nearly fifteen pounds on an already slight frame. Mother scooped her gangly baby into her arms and fled home, lips drawn tight the entire two-hour drive.

They would try again, twice, at last settling for a large yellow clapboard Victorian in the Delaware countryside, staffed by a couple with their own disabled child. They called it a group home, and home it was, with dogs and a real kitchen, living room, and bedrooms for the kids though they were some odd-looking kids, moaning and scraping around the basketball court.

Years went by. I left for college, graduate school, and soon after began a family with a good man and two healthy daughters of my own. No one faulted me for keeping my distance. My sisters and I have always been war-veteran close. To blow off steam, we allowed ourselves politically incorrect jokes about the retarded. We ran the other direction when spotting a group of them on field trips. We stewed, we mourned, or none of the above. There was unspoken forgiveness for whatever tack we chose in dealing with Boo. Outsiders were the ones who misunderstood, who saw my inattention as uncaring. Most likely their experience was confined to the mildly retarded, those with greater awareness and independence. There was the question of whether Boo even *knew* us.

When I was nearly forty, my eldest asked to meet her aunt, the only aunt she'd never seen. She was curious, so we drove out to Beckie's school, where we were escorted down a long hallway to a shoebox in the back, with windows all around. We found her strapped into a chair, coated in chocolate and saliva, bellowing with clear satisfaction. I could feel Laura back away, full of concerns I would need to address. But for a few minutes, I spoke to my sister, clucked and murmured in that lilting soprano you would use to address an infant. I touched her corkscrew hair. She leaned her head against my shoulder, scanning my face with those wayward eyes. Seeing her raised a river of tenderness and murk. Were the nurses treating her well? Did they know she drank from a plastic cup, never glass, and adored highly processed smoked turkey?

Because she chewed imperfectly and frequently inhaled her food, Beckie was prone to pneumonia. She bounced back from one terrible case after another, beating the odds in spite of scarring, weakness, and dire prognosis. Once in the ICU, we made the tormented decision to remove her from the respirator, and we gathered at her bedside to say good-bye. As if on cue, she immediately resumed breathing on her own. But we knew these farewells were practice, and indeed, when she turned forty-one, a particularly ferocious infection finally took her life.

I've heard that while we are in utero, we may be accompanied by the undeveloped cells of a ghost twin. Grieving for Beckie has felt like this. She is a shadow-life tucked under my body-eaves. There she sways with her lopsided limbs, rickrack teeth, and gentle infant demeanor. She ties me to the earth, my little instructor, reminding me never to feel completely safe or too full of pride. She is my discomfiting, my never-never-land little sister.

On Lying

I'll come clean, right now. I excused my daughter's absence from school with a lie. We wanted to get a jump on our vacation, so I told Sister Paulette that Bonnie would be attending her great-uncle Max's funeral on Friday. Indeed, he had passed away last winter, the touch of truth that made the lie easier. It takes some chutzpah to lie to a nun, though people of all ages have been doing it for years.

What did I feel? About twelve years old, like one of the girls roaming around me in their hiked-up blue skirts.

But I was determined, with a specific purpose in mind: we would leave early for the long drive to Door County, avoiding late-afternoon traffic. Bonnie's commitment to her classes and Sister Paulette were the only obstacles. My lie, like most lies, was a method of achieving my goal. Our goal, my family's goal, that of expediency or safety or however I justified it at the time.

I was also careful, perhaps more so than the uniformed teenagers around me. After all, I was replacing the truth with a falsehood and it had to be believable, with characters, details, motivation. Believable, but simple; I couldn't imagine myself reciting an elaborate story, sustaining that kind of false energy.

Liars should have good memories.
—PROVERB

Later, after I was well rested and back in my routine of dropping Bonnie off at school, seeing her safely inside, then leaving for work, Sister Paulette pulled me aside. We sat together under the bronze crucifix and sentimental portrait of Our Savior, the office a whirlwind of bells, buzzers, and flicked ponytails. I wondered if the school was bankrupt and she was breaking the news to each parent individually. Or maybe Bonnie was in trouble of some kind. I was alert and confused. Sister Paulette held my hands in hers and peered directly into my pupils, as if to check for shrinkage. She whispered, "I'm so sorry for your loss."

Loss. My chin dropped. I glanced to the left, hoping to recover my bearings, felt a pilot light catch under my skin and heat climb. I had forgotten all about the long-suffering uncle. My response came after a long pause, during which time I was frantically searching my back-up files. "Sorry for your loss," I repeated. "Oh, that loss. Well, he was a distant uncle. We were not very close to him."

Sister Paulette saw it all. If she hadn't been 100 percent confident before, she must have noticed my relief when the subject changed, and we began to discuss the "air-conditioned county" in Wisconsin where we relaxed and recreated. If I had been telling the truth, I might have been a bit more eager to return to the theme. A woman who has lost someone wears her grief like a plus-size coat: her skin droops, her shoulders slide. I was refreshed after my two-weeks-and-a-day vacation and rather perky.

The body never lies. In its collusion with the truth, it avoids eye contact, limits movement of arms and hands. The liar is not likely to touch her chest, but fidgets a lot, grazing face, throat, hair. She backs up in her chair, sits stiffly, compresses her physical space. Timing and duration of emotional gestures are also slightly off–too short or late. When a liar is faking emotion–delight or grief–her facial expressions can't really get into it. Eyebrows furrow as if a fly were in the air, a smile's confined to the lips instead of the whole face.

Aphasics, who have lost the ability to speak or understand language, quickly develop an acute sensitivity to physical gesture. They are among the best lie detectors, reports Nancy L. Etcoff, and others, in *Nature* magazine. They pick up all their clues from watching a liar move rather than listening to her speech.

My mother too was gifted with an unusually keen social intelligence, or "shit detector," as she called it. She distrusted Phil Donahue, and G. Gordon Liddy *before* the Watergate scandal broke. Though Lutheran by baptism, she had a Jewish impatience with niceties, euphemisms, whitewashing, and could see from a mile away whether someone was faking it.

This made my adolescence difficult. To honor my curfew, I went to my room at eleven, locked my door, climbed onto a chair under the window, cranked the handle, squeezed through, and dropped to the begonias below. Then I'd walk briskly to the bridge by Mohegan and Goldsboro, where my boyfriend stood smoking under haloed streetlights. Night after night after night, our relationship secretly flourished.

Weeding the side yard one hot afternoon, my mother spotted the crushed flowers. I blurted out an explanation: "It must have been those dogs. A whole pack of them. Look what they've done!" We both knew the real story. To my mother, it wasn't worth the fight, so nothing surfaced, little changed, except perhaps my avoidance of her begonias when I leapt into the steamy dark.

In common use from the fourteenth all the way up to the seventeenth century was the adjective *gull*, of Germanic origin, which meant, "yellow or pale." The noun *gull* referred to "an unfledged bird, especially a gosling." A young, inexperienced bird, pale and yellow, might be easily deceived. From this comes the word *gullible*.

Though pale, Sister Paulette was no fledgling bird, sparrow nor goose. Neither was my mother.

Kindness should override truth.
—SAMUEL BUTLER

I don't think my parents ever lied to me. The worst I remember is a kind of imprecision. When asked about the results of my IQ test, my mom responded, "Oh, somewhere between your father's and mine." I could tell, in the name of tenderness, she allowed herself a white lie, a clean cloth over a knotty table. I was satisfied with her answer and sat like a sparrow, safe between my parents on the swaying intelligence wire.

The truth is often too hurtful, terrifying, unpleasant, mundane, or confusing to deal with. It begs embellishment. As a consequence, in varying degrees, for multiple reasons lying is an essential element of social interaction. Here are four points on a possibly infinite list of examples:

- Joni Mitchell doesn't wear makeup: "Not really. A little blush, concealer, a dash of mascara, a little color on the lips. And that's it." Joni wants us to think her beauty is effortless. The *Times* calls this "makeup denial."
- Please do not call them McMansions. They are "luxury estates," a phrase that conjures up Versailles, Fontainebleau, Kensington Gardens in the dappled, rolling hills of France or England. For a mere $5 or 6 million, you too can be a count, lord or lady, prince or princess from a long line of blue bloods.
- The director promises to get you started in the very next play, scheduled for spring. When you don't sleep with him, the part never materializes; you can't even get him on the phone.
- "I did not have sexual relations with that woman," said President Clinton. Note his avoidance of the contraction "didn't," as well as his reference to "that woman," formalizing, and distancing himself from Monica Lewinsky. Thousands of teenagers are now "abstaining from sex" by practicing fellatio. This benefits boys in particular, a happy new population of Little Bills.

A lie is a social tool. We lie to avoid consequences—hurting the feelings of a loved one, embarrassment, failure, impeachment, jail, or sometimes just because it's easier than relaying the complicated truth. (I borrowed the sweater from my sister who borrowed it from her roommate who bought it at a thrift shop. Or: Thank you. I don't remember where I got it.) We also lie to get something we want, whether it is a fluffier version of our lackluster selves, a longer vacation, membership in some elite intellectual group, or a house in the Pacific Palisades.

Even animals will lie. Our hound dog Emma sleeps on the living room couch; it's her spot, her kingdom. When her sibling Monty hops up there before her, she rushes to the front door to let roll her mellifluous, hound-dog bellow. There is, of course, no intruder. We all know she's faking, except Monty, who jumps off the couch to join in the fray. Who can blame him? It's the wolf's cry, the irresistible bugle call of the hunt. He's bewitched and falls for it every time. As soon as he lands on all fours, Emma stops barking abruptly and leaps onto the couch before Monty knows what hit him.

There are some cases where lying is a virtue in the animal kingdom. Consider the nesting plover who spots a predator and immediately begins an elaborate charade of limping, squealing, dragging and dipping of one supposedly broken wing toward an adjacent sand dune and away from her brood. Animals dissemble for many of the same reasons we do. Monty's hair rises along his spine and he grows two inches taller. A magnificent frigate bird puffs up its scarlet feathers until its throat is bigger than a bear's heart. Plants too: The mountain laurel's pollen-coated, spring-loaded stamens are painted a bright, alluring pink. From scent and color, the lady-slipper creates a tantalizing canoe-shaped trap for bees and spiders.

Rocks and cement do not lie. The very idea is absurd. It appears the lie is a characteristic of living things, an extension of

Darwinian notions of natural selection. The liar, whether plant or animal, casts a spell for a handful of reasons: to jump-start the reproductive process, protect its young, defend its territory, escape predation, scare or intimidate rivals, or otherwise appear more fit in the world's eye.

> *The most enchanting things in nature*
> *and art are based on deception.*
> —VLADIMIR NABOKOV

Here is a poem that describes a deception gone wild, from Jeffrey Harrison's collection *Feeding the Fire*:

OUR OTHER SISTER

The cruelest thing I did to my younger sister
wasn't shooting a homemade blowdart into her knee,
where it dangled for a breathless second

before dropping off, but telling her we had
another, older sister who'd gone away.
What my motives were I can't recall: a whim,

or was it some need of mine to toy with loss,
to probe the ache of imaginary wounds?
But that first sentence was like a string of DNA

that replicated itself in coiling lies
when my sister began asking her desperate questions.
I called our older sister Isabel

and gave her hazel eyes and long blonde hair.
I had her run away to California
where she took drugs and made hippie jewelry.

Before I knew it, she'd moved to Santa Fe
and opened a shop. She sent a postcard
every year or so, but she'd stopped calling.

I can still see my younger sister staring at me,
her eyes widening with desolation
then filling with tears. I can still remember

how thrilled and horrified I was
that something I'd just made up
had that kind of power, and I can just feel

the blowdart of remorse stabbing me in the heart
as I rushed to tell her none of it was true.
But it was too late. Our other sister

had already taken shape, and we could not
call her back from her life far away
or tell her how badly we missed her.

The first false sentence the speaker recalls in this poem–the
pronouncement and vague shape of another sister–is the eas-
iest. But a lie is seldom solitary; it begs another and another,
until an imaginary skeleton is built, bone by bone, muscle and
flesh, a sister-hologram with hobbies, home, hair. The greater
the detail, the less likely she will crumble. The longer her history, the greater the strain, until he can't even make the truth
believable and must suffer "the blowdart of remorse."

Initially, the speaker lies to get what he wants. Perhaps it began with a whim. Or big-brother meanness, like the homemade
blowdart. Perhaps indeed the speaker was "toying with loss,"
or probing "the ache of imaginary wounds." Whatever the motivation, the lie flatters the liar. Like Joni Mitchell's makeup
denial or the frigate bird's magnificent feathers, the lie allows
him "that kind of power."

True consciousness, the recognition of self, separated from
world, occurs at around age seven, the age at which a child
also begins to lie. Teenagers are notorious liars. They lie about
their whereabouts, drugs and alcohol, school attendance,
grades, boyfriends, sex, mostly to avoid punishment from
various authority figures. But they lie to their friends as well,
boosting their intelligence, sexual experience, cool quotient.
The high social pressure of adolescence makes them desperate for any and every kind of "spell." It is often a way of *being*.
Bonnie once told her teacher she had been abused and now her
parents were divorcing. She noticed how victims were getting
all the attention, their status clearly elevated to the point of ce-
lebrity. Again, we were pulled into the Sister's office as the first
step in a kind of intervention. We could see the open training
manual on her desk, as well as a Xeroxed list of professional
counselors.

Perhaps lying follows the natural curve of a child's independence—my lie makes me NOT YOU. My lie makes me ME. Human beings are not ants who, lifelong, remain committed to
their basic job description. We have the ability to depart from

communal dependence. The lie, whether to avoid or get something, is the primitive beginning of the effort to distinguish oneself.

~~⁓~~

Like most young people, I experimented with a variety of personas, from Amazonian firefighter to urban botanist to country schoolteacher. Only the poet stuck, but even then, in order to write poems, I faked masculinity. I dressed in jeans and a flannel shirt, sat at a table swept clean of comforting objects. Then I imagined how a guy would see the mule grazing in my front yard, the piles of rotten Osage oranges, dirt road winding out to our mailbox, and grackles decimating the few tomatoes left in our garden. I feigned confidence. My voice deepened and I began to write, using description as a way in.

Back then, this maleness was where most of the published works came from, where the good ideas lived, or so it seemed. My poems had almost nothing to do with my true life; they were chill, disembodied fabrications. But I believed in them, and they were successful, published in prestigious literary magazines.

Not long after, I married and had a baby–a colicky no-sleeper whose very existence squashed my conceit like an egg carton. Pretend to be a man, when your entire body is in service to a famished child, a female at her functional peak? After three years of this, I hardly recognized the person who had written my poems. It was absurd, even impossible to lie, to play the cowboy again and pick up where I left off. I began a slow crawl back to some semblance of honesty in my work, and then to publish these poems at the level I had before. Now I partition off my identity, using my maiden or "professional" name for poems and essays, my married name for church newsletters and legal documents, and a little bit of both for my work in publishing. This fits right in with shifting notions of the self. We are made of *many* selves, not just one. Over a lifetime, we float between honesty and fabrication, between conformity–our dependence on others–and the urge to be separate from them. Maybe the natural truth *is* dependence and the denial of it necessary for us to accomplish anything beyond basic survival.

In Harrison's poem the speaker lies to his sister, his incentive a whim or cruelty or the need to appear larger than life, like the magnificent frigate bird. But what of the poem itself? Is the writer telling the truth? Was there a sister at all, trusting and loyal? If not, what are the writer's motives in deceiving us? What can we make of this enchantment inside an enchantment, writing that casts a spell on the reader too?

The con man may employ wit and cleverness in his scam, but his lie remains a poor man's lie, with close ties to evolutionary pressure. His enchantment is basic and blunt. Freud would place the artist only slightly above the criminal. In his assessment, the artist "desires to win honor, power, wealth, fame, and the love of women."

But art is not solely a form of greed and self-aggrandizement. Harrison's poem, by the nature of its medium, will never bring him more than a few dollars. At best, a successful poem will garner a thousand extra readers, hardly the legions of adoring fans that flock to rock concerts. Doesn't the artist also:

Compose a suite of songs to remember, or reactivate some past music in herself? Paint to safeguard the view from a farmhouse window, visualize a betrayal, pleasure, loss? Write to understand, clarify, generalize, move from the micro to the macro, the personal to the public, like a set of Russian nesting dolls opened in reverse? Artists play with reality, whether they manipulate language, paint, or a digital camera. Call it poetic license, embellishment, or outright lying, they are loose in their allegiance to facts. How interesting that the word *fact* comes from the Latin *factum*, "to do or make." It's the same root for *artifice, counterfeit, facade, facsimile*. Icarus's wings did not melt when he defied the warning and flew close to the sun. A princess cannot really feel a pea under dozens of mattresses. Artists prevaricate in order to tell the truth.

Here's another poem (mine), rife with deception:

HOMESICKNESS

On another continent, mother circles the farmhouse.
She steams gnocchi, tosses them in butter.

Mother and daughter have matching teeth, like a zipper.

If daughter flies home she'll lose eight hours. If her car were amphibious,
the loss would be hardly perceptible.

There's always the mail. And the cell phone, like a human cowbell.
Especially if you are loved.

Mother rings her from the bus stop, train station, grocery
store.

When it's time to pay, she says hang on. The bus pulls up,
gotta go, so long!

Emotion: from the Latin *emovere*–to move away, "in
transport."

How would a jet land in the country, gravel roads
and all those electric fences?

She opens her mail, a blue mountain of *Mit Luftpost, Par
Avion*.

Genes are a kind of blue letter from a mother
to her daughter: Good news, bad news.

What is a mother but a tooth's way of producing another
tooth?

My mother never lived in a farmhouse; she was raised in
suburban Milwaukee. My mother and I do not have matching
teeth. The zipper came first as an image of connection/discon-
nection; our teeth match only in the sense that all teeth match,
although I had braces and she did not. It is not true my mother
rings me on the fly, in fact, cell phones did not exist during her
lifetime. "What is a mother," I conclude, "but a tooth's way
of producing another tooth?" This is a rather cold statement
stumbled on by fusing genetic "blue letters" and those matching teeth–a drastic reduction of a mother's role, true to the
poem, true perhaps of some mothers, but definitely not true of
mine.

Asked about the origins of poetry, Nabokov responded, "When a cave boy came running back to the cave, through the tall grass, shouting as he ran, 'Wolf, wolf,' and there *was* no wolf, his baboonlike parents, great sticklers for the truth, gave him a hiding, no doubt, but poetry had been born–the tall story had been born in the tall grass." Tall tales, yarns, fish stories– there are many names for this sort of lie. But in most cases, the motives are similar: to entertain, yes, but also to get at a truth the facts won't allow. Perhaps lying has, by its narrow definition, been given a bad name. Maybe Ulysses is an elaborate lie, originating on the same ground as the Mafia don denying the assassination of an entire family. The difference is complexity and, of course, motivation. The Mafioso's lie is simple survival. The lying artist hints at a deeper definition of self and a greater organization of the world. My lie to the nun was pure greed and selfish desire.

Sister Paulette wore an indigo habit of the modern style, skirt just below the knee, sensible shoes. She was sturdy and moved nimbly for someone her age. I couldn't help but notice she'd sprung for the more expensive graduated lenses for her wire-rimmed glasses. After years spent absorbing and dodging various crises, demands, and fibs, she was a solid combination of common sense, spiritual discipline, and perhaps the slightest hint of vanity.

Or, there were no graduated lenses, no sensible shoes, indeed, no Paulette or Catholic school. Like Harrison, I have designed a sister-hologram with language and imagination, instead of bone and blood–all inventions to dramatize the story, to underscore the flagrancy of a lie and its uncomfortable consequences. Perhaps Bonnie went to a huge public school with an overworked staff and a multitude of misbehaving students. Perhaps we picked her up as usual on Thursday and hit the road early the next morning. Her absence on Friday would hardly have been noticed. It doesn't really matter. I'm almost not sure myself after all these years—a lifetime of truths, lies, truths that turned out to be lies, lies that turned out to be true. It's all part of the effort to explain what I'm doing here, on earth.

PER *f* E C T
Water

A tricolored flag from west harbor to east dock. Near stripe of amber, middle aquamarine, finally black with touches of evergreen. So clear, so spotless this early in the season, too cold for human swimming. Presumably fished out, though every day a man wades out to seduce a smallmouth bass.

A dinghy named *Pesto* zigzags through the water. Zig. Zag. The rower can't see behind, where she is going. She steers toward Anderson's buoy, avoids the deep and also the shallow where stones would gouge into the boat. Her oars give warning—clank, scrape, jerk—instead of the smooth glide forward. She marks her progress against the shore, past boat docks, sagging green cabins, and the ancient Trollhaugen guesthouse.

She's not even a little wet but feels like she's taking a giant bath of peridots, a gemwater rinse from scalp to toe. Her boat leaves a meandering wake of darker emerald trimmed with foam. The oars send off tiny whirlpools on both sides. Sometimes she stops to watch their retreat, how they chase each other, then flatten, barely five feet out, and blend into the current. The sound is hushed and delicious and makes her mouth water. It's tempting to take a drink, so she lowers her hand, holds it under till her fingers go numb.

Next year, she'll arrive later in the summer when the water's temperate, better for swimming, but laced with bits of algae that slither across her ankles.

So it goes with perfect: its anchor drifts, catches again in time, some other immaculate place.

Marking Time in
Door County

I'm sitting on the pier, first morning of our ten-day vacation. Green Bay is in party mode. Whitecaps collide and dance from crisscrossing wakes. Pontoon boats putter along, their riders squawking like chicks in aluminum baskets. I breathe in the odor of juniper, mown grass, beer, and yes, alewives, a dozen of them, curled and bloated inside the marina. A storm's on its way, but sky-wise, there's only a distant smudge of cloud over Horseshoe Island. Inside the house the girls are waking up– Laura at the fridge, Bonnie rummaging for her hairbrush, best friend Kristin humming in the shower. A fly finds its way to the honey at the bottom of my teacup.

Ten thousand such mornings have passed since my grandparents purchased a house called Gray Logs, with a lean-to kitchen and 150 feet of waterfront in Ephraim, Wisconsin. In 1947 the village held a few rustic hotels, an ice-cream shop, and Anderson's dock with its graffiti-clogged barn. American Indians, the French, and Norwegians were among Ephraim's early visitors. We are the latest, one of fourteen third- and fourth-generation families who now share this property with its Scandinavian log buildings, its hemlocks and swamp, its flocks of mallards and gulls. We come from all over the country–Maryland, Kentucky, Idaho, California, and New York–to ground more constant and welcoming than the fourteen places we call home.

The approach from Highway 42 winds through Egg Harbor, Fish Creek, Ephraim, and finally, to Gray Logs, at the bottom of a deeply shadowed driveway. Then the sky opens out and water fills in the spaces. We can see Horseshoe Island, Eagle Bluff, and remarkably, Three Sisters Islands, several miles away over swells and sails. No streetlights or lane markers here. And the trees are not the kind I worry about in my own backyard, yellowing and sparse. They are grand, gracious ladies in evergreen dresses; they are here to soothe, to whisper reassurances. Stendhal defined beauty as "the promise of happiness." I walk out onto the rickety pier and let the wind with its odor of grass and Green Bay hit me from all sides. It's possible when this idea occurred to him, Stendhal was standing in just such a place.

My grandparents are here too, invisible comfort, solicitous ghosts. One waving from the kitchen, the other still in bed with her tray of coffee and toast. They traveled the world but always returned, for there was no place they found lovelier than Gray Logs. My husband and I sleep in their room, shower in their once off-limits-to-kids bathroom. Though decades have passed since they died, it feels a little bit like trespassing. The girls have staked out the upstairs. We make short shrift of unpacking, and with bathing suits under our shorts and water shoes in hand, the celebration begins.

No swimming for me, not just yet. I have a ritual I must attend to on every visit. I say hello to the house by kissing the smooth gray banister, by shedding my shoes and running my toes over the flagstones, by opening the linen closet and counting the blue-and-white-striped towels.

I'm expressing my thanks for safe arrival. Not just this one in 2002, but all my arrivals. Here on the braided living room rug, center of the house, where everything is stored, no whisper or footstep is excluded. I listen, breathe deeply, sniff for the raucous poker games on the folding card table, red and blue plastic chips careening about like unsure bicycles, Bicycle cards leaping when John or Chuck or Nan slam down a faux-furious fist. The sweep of our grandfather's terrycloth robe, his tray of perfect over-easies and sausage. And my father vexing the floorboards with early morning back stretches and leg lifts, creaking inside the body and out. I touch the maroon slip-covered sofa. Down into the fibers I go like a medical detective, uncovering wet towels, shed bathing suits, the crumpled wrappers of great-grandfather's red anise, which he used to lure us little ones closer until we hated the candies, even as adults. He was too old and his forehead too shiny. Between the polished floor planks went 221 baby fingers picking up lost cinnamon imperials. I inhale the dander from Scotties and Westies, bassets, pointers, and mutts. Thirty-nine years of no-see-ums, yellow jackets, and dust.

I say hello to the house and then I'm ready for a swim, one of many this August, with its record heat. The water level rises and falls, depending on snowfall and conditions north in Lake Superior. We've seen the rocky beach grow by a hundred feet or, worse, waves lap at the solarium windows. There was talk then of moving the house back, but my grandmother, with her second sight, was adamant—wait, she said, it *will* recede. Now we slip and stumble over the rocks to reach deep water, that creamy green-black essence like liquid malachite.

I wonder if the experience of time varies, like metabolism, in relation to a creature's size. A second may be long in the life of the horsefly, buzzing around my head, affecting everything from the rate of a vibration to holding that exact angle as it approaches my naked stretch of blood-delicious skin. For humans there is infinite variability: dashing-dream-and-movie time, suffering-pain-bored-ugly-chore time, when we are aware of every second ticking. Long ago, the Chinese maintained two separate official calendars, one for the peasant, which followed the seasons, and one for the scribe, a pure number system. At home we are scribes, rousing in the dark to the numeral 6 and a sound like a security breach. But here we are peasants relishing food, water, and blankets under the skies. We have unplugged the digital clocks. The tarnished mantel clock chimes capriciously. Time to rise when the sun reaches the Swedish painted bed. Time to swim when it soaks the glassed-in porch and the breezeway is thick and still. Time for dinner when "counter-twilight," a reflection of the sunset in rust and purple, appears in the east. We sit happily in one minute, two, three, as the earth rotates and colors drain from the sky.

I think of my vacation as a miniature lifespan. During the first wide-eyed days, like the first weeks of a newborn, time is sluggish, even static. The nurturing first breakfast–oatmeal and cream, or pancakes with fresh-picked raspberries–stretches on forever. We wrap our arms around the kids, around each other. There are long, luxurious hours till lunch. We can bike to the park *and* run to town for batteries. A nap feels like a full night's sleep. So lapses Monday and Tuesday and Wednesday. The girls have occupied the roof with cushions and towels, their tanning salon. I nibble at my novel.

I've brought with me two–one is a classic (family requirement), Fitzgerald's *Tender Is the Night*. The other's contemporary, Paula Fox's *Poor George*. *George* is tough going for its creepy claustrophobia. Still, I dawdle and sigh over Fox's taut observations: "Her feet swelled like muffins through the open spaces of her suede sandals." Fitzgerald brings the sea into every line: "Simultaneously, the whole party moved toward the water, super-ready from the long, forced inaction, passing from the heat to the cool with the gourmandise of a tingling curry eaten with chilled white wine." Fox seems brown, clotted, and thick. Fitzgerald is turquoise and swift, but perhaps that's because he comes second, later in the trip.

It is a known phenomenon that long periods of time appear to pass more rapidly as people grow older. There's a logical explanation: one day to an eleven-year-old is roughly 1/4,000 of her life, while the same twenty-four hours to a fifty-five-year-old is approximately 1/20,000 of her life. The measure of time itself remains constant. But here, even a preteen notices the hours are striding along at a conspicuous clip. By midvacation, the morning seems not so sumptuous or full. We say it's because we slept in later. We say the book reads quickly because we are more relaxed, more able to concentrate. But the girls know better, and they are itchy.

So we get serious, determined to cover all the bases, to squeeze in as much fun as possible. Two trips to the drive-in, one on Thursday, and one Monday, to catch both movies but avoid the crowds. Cancel the Farm because the drive's too long and, really, aren't we too old to be cradling kittens and baby goats? Climb Eagle Tower on the way to Little Sister Beach and pay only one parking fee. And malts, Wilson's incredible vanilla malts every night, brought down to the dock to watch the bay swallow the sun, inch by inch.

The Koine Greek word for "beautiful" derives from the word ὥρα, *hōra*, meaning "hour." Beauty was thus associated with "being of one's hour," as in a perfectly ripe cantaloupe, or a sunset at its absolute peak. Can you imagine freezing this moment, or having it all at once–a lifetime of sunsets, each slightly unique, layered one on the other, compounded till their beauty, and our experience of it, breaks down? Thank goodness the earth withholds, gives us twenty-four hours to forget, so we return each evening with a relatively fresh pair of eyes. Thank goodness for the gift of finitude, just right for this particular instant.

Alas, the second set of Monday, Tuesday, and Wednesday seems like an abridged version of the first. One trip to the grocery store for grape juice and the entire afternoon seems to evaporate. Kristin and Bonnie have finished their required reading assignments, and Bonnie is satisfied with her tan. She pulls me into the bathroom to show me, and at first I think she's wearing a white bikini. Sadness and anxiety begin to creep in; we find ourselves less in the present, making arrangements for our departure, jealous of the next family that, like clockwork, will drive down the driveway on Thursday morning to displace us.

Yes, there were summers we drummed our fingers, anxious for the arrival of Family B with their horns tooting, kayaks roped to the car roof. Two weeks of rain and a pair of miserable phlegmy toddlers were an endurance test; only six hundred miles and we could drop them off at their grandparents'! Another year, my husband made the decision to quit smoking where it was beautiful and stress-free. . . . And later, that night-owl couple we invited along in '88. I've never been so exhausted. But these were exceptions; mostly we looked for ways to extend the pleasure.

I had the idea that if I chose the right object, I could bring my vacation home. Oh, I know, fortunes have been made on souvenirs that in the French allow one "to recall" places and in the Latin "to come to mind." But, I reasoned, the tchotchkes sold in gift shops all over Door Peninsula were impersonal and expensive–painted ducks, quilted hot pads, the shrink-wrapped dried cherries for four dollars an ounce. Nothing like our own tasteful, hand-worn, sponge-glazed mugs that had traveled through four generations of mothers, aunts, nieces, sons, their hot cocoa stains old enough to withstand the strongest bleach. Here was our history, Gray Logs itself, compact enough to slip into a pocket.

I discovered a beautiful lace doily in a deep drawer under placemats and tablecloths, work that simply isn't done anymore. My grandmother must have kept a dozen of these in her city house. No one will miss it, I thought. Sheepishly, I folded it into quarters and tucked it into my suitcase. But at home, the doily rested uneasily on dresser top, desk, dining room table, till finally I stuffed it back in my drawer for its safe return back to Wisconsin.

Wittgenstein noticed that when the human eye sees something beautiful, the hand wants to draw it. Elaine Scarry begins her ingenious study *On Beauty and Being Just* with this idea. She describes a "forward momentum," how beauty incites the desire to bring new things into the world: babies, drawings, photographs, poems, and so on.

With a similar noble intention, I inaugurated the obligatory-or-not Guest Book–record of bliss, something to touch and savor, which could be revisited again and again. It would double as a conversation between families, across time slots! August in

Ephraim, June in Ephraim. Family B and their enormous clan; Family A, who preferred to be alone; Family C, who politely tolerated Family A. The little green book would stitch all of us back together again.

In practice though, the entries were awkward. Long lists of activities–identical activities from year to year, family to family–miniature golf at the Red Putter, rowing to Anderson's dock, biking, ferries to Washington Island. Budding young writers contributed purple accounts of water and sailboats. There were tributes to the generosity of our matriarch and patriarch. Once in a while, something unusual happened. An exploding wasp nest, a muzzle full of porcupine quills–these stories scratched in ten-year-old scrawl. But five or six years went by and the entries fizzled out. It was a chore to chronicle a perfect swim under Eagle Bluff, when after all, the reader could just go there and swim herself.

On the last evening of our vacation, a front moves through, bringing a Canadian chill and raucous wind. All night the curtains suck and swell. The big gray-planked doors with their wrought-iron hardware unhitch and slam. In a few hours, the temperature drops twenty degrees. Family B and their guests are the lucky ones now; they'll get that "air-conditioned county" thrill. Our backpacks are lined up in the hall, bike rack strapped on the car, and the cooler ready to go. I'm hardly here anymore, projecting myself South, two hundred miles down Route 42, 43, 90, 65 toward home and the mail at work.

My good-byes are not so sensual as my hellos. I narrow them down to three stations–the pier, kitchen, surrounding spruces, hemlocks, and white pines. All get a brisk "See you next year." Then I turn my back on the thousands of beloved details: the blue enamel mugs, the cast-iron dachshund by the front door, the rowboat, seatless, splintery, battered by cousins and uncles and severe Wisconsin cold. I turn my back on my grandparents too, whose death feels a little too close right now.

It's small compensation, but our subconscious lags a few days behind real time. This means that the benefits of vacation do linger, more than just physically. Sure, we'll be more relaxed, able to bear that crisis at work or school with greater flexibility and confidence. Better yet, we'll have a cache of dreams that plays out deliciously, of cherry pie and inner tubes, the stony beach, and wide open skies and water. For a while, we'll feel like we're still breathing pure northern air, our ancestors close by, and sleep is a serene cove we gladly swim into.

P E R *f* E C T
Solution

A toddler's pink-and-white-striped dress, with gauzy apron, and purple-ribbon tiebacks. Hand-me-down from her cousin, already well worn, nevertheless worn every day whether or not her mother would allow it. The dress had a name–"Pollo," like "Paulo," a close derivative of "pillow," for she slept inside the dress, not needing a pillow. On the yoke, two oval strawberry stains and one long drip of indeterminate origin. Apron semi-detached in places, where she stepped on it while attempting to rise from a sitting position.

It was a slip of mother, like her mother's slip, a second skin without the hurting patches. She lifted the dress over her face and her stomach calmed. She lowered it and knew what to do next. Could you wear a pillow, a glowworm, a blanket? The dress was her forest place without the scary journey.

She listened to the dress and, in time, refused to wear anything else. In her parents' world, this was impossible. What would people think–that she was poor, unbeloved? They cajoled, distracted her with party shoes, firmly enforced time-outs when the battle grew intense, and still the child would not take off the dress.

What is the perfect solution but a pair of disappointments, two less-than-perfects, a middle-making. Not throwing the dress away, not wearing it forever. What, said her father, if Pollo were a pet, like parakeet or fish? Would you crush it in your sleep? Wouldn't you want to pat, preserve, and keep it happy?

She could have her dress, but only if she carried it in a brown paper bag. And so she did for five years, and then some.

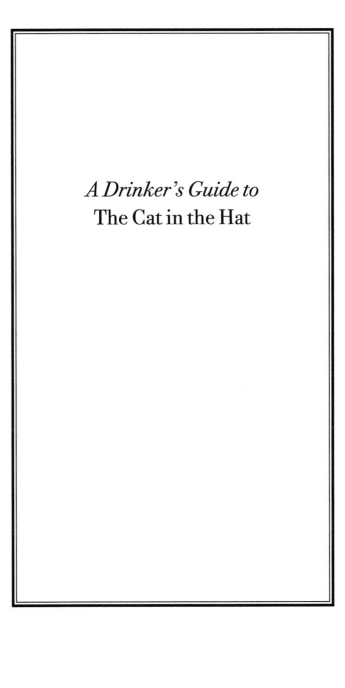

A Drinker's Guide to
The Cat in the Hat

He taught at a community college in rural Maryland, an evening class in introductory literature that ended at ten p.m. The commute home was an hour over single-lane highways to another small town in nearby Delaware. But first . . . a package store for a six-pack and a pint of Seagram's. The drive home was cool and black and empty of traffic. Blinking yellow lights at most intersections, a few lit farmhouses, and once in a while a long low chicken barn, set back discreetly from the road, so the smell wouldn't overwhelm. He sipped Seagram's from the bottle, washing it down with beer.

His edges wore down slowly. The mechanics of clutch, accelerator, and brake were liquid, headlights spanning into ditches and deep pasture. Even Christian rock was sweet at this speed. On his way to distinct inebriation, he savored the leather grip, the steering wheel swaying along with the music, eyes drifting rather than darting from field to road, stoplight to dashboard.

Remember the story about a girl who crashed when she leaned forward to adjust the radio dial? Fiddling with a rear-view mirror was just as dangerous: *Eyes on the road, driver.* Thinking himself vigilant, he slowed way too early for an intersection many yards away. Brake lights ahead were doubled, though the left-hand set rarely stayed still, stretching, retracting. Like Turkish taffy, he observed.

By the time he steered his wagon onto Market Street and pulled into our narrow driveway at 1611, he was radiating, blood a low purr. Up the steep stairs, one hand, sometimes two, on the pipe handrail to the second floor apartment, where his wife and two young daughters slept in three tiny bedrooms.

We slid into deeper sleep when his book bag slumped into the captain's chair. He was home.

~~~

Something goes BUMP, the cat hits the door, head or hat misjudging, or perhaps it is only the door itself slamming into the wall.

The children are seated by the window, the weather chill and rainy, not at all conducive to imaginative play. They startle, lifting an inch off their butts. Even the curtains jump, and then the door swings open.

Not a straight line on him. He doesn't appear to have a skeleton! Hat beating his foot inside the door, it leans that far forward. Did he roll out of bed, tail like a mangled pipe cleaner, forgetting to shed his jammies and put on something more presentable? Why isn't the cat at work, doing something constructive? On two legs he lurches in, tipping his hat, balancing his drippy umbrella on the end of his thumb. He knows some games; he has saved up a bunch of tricks to make a great day. This cat brings *fun*; he doesn't care if mother is out running errands or a meeting, or anything else.

~~~

"Come on . . ." he pleaded, proposing on our honeymoon that we blow several hundred on a meal at Harry's Bar and then sip a bottle of wine on a gondola ride through Venice's back canals. Seventy dollars for a half-hour! Under this bridge, duck, quick. Let's go for more! The curried sole with polenta, the lazy dark, sonic with far-off festivity, and a traffic jam made of boats. But to tell the truth, twenty-five years later that's what we remember, little more.

Italy seeded a taste for motorcycles too, and though I protested it was groceries we were burning, he bought a bright red Vespa with matching helmets. Scents and temperature brightened unlike anything we'd known in a car. Lilac! Manure! Fried chicken! We dipped into a gully like a glass of ice water, took the full hit of a mown lawn, though I warned him to avoid the shavings, shouting through my face mask and the wind. Conversation was ridiculous, riding was risky, but it was a magnificent thrill.

Happy to play the fool in shrill animal voices the children loved (Wamu the Jamaican rag doll rescued from a burning building by Purpley the stuffed elephant, who stretched out his trunk so she could slide down), he performed mesmerizing dramas without the soggy moral or neat conclusion. Sure his face was a little too red like he was about to pop. Sure there was something disquieting in all that energy. Dads were supposed to be grown-ups. But yes, yes, another game, another game! He gave each girl a full glass of water, filled his mouth, and exploded in a spit-take. Soon they were feeding each other knock-knock jokes, bursting before the punch line was out, soaked and drooling. He bought seven cans of shaving cream on Halloween and they decorated the rhododendrons, gleefully appearing later with sprayed-on beards, scary eyebrows, and beehive hairdos.

According to the company's literature, over 370 million cases of Seagram's Seven have been sold since 1934, giving this brand the distinction of being consumed more often than any other brand of whiskey in the history of the United States. The ingredients list is straightforward—corn, rye, rye malt, barley malt, yeast, and water. The corn comes exclusively from fields in Indiana, while the other grains are imported from farms in the Midwest. The name "whiskey" is a Gaelic translation of the Latin phrase *aqua vitae*, meaning "water of life." Seagram's was the favored drink of "Dimebag" Darrell Abbott, a heavy-metal guitarist before he was murdered onstage by a fan. Dimebag mixed his Seagram's with a shot of Crown Royal and a splash of Coke, a drink he called "Black Tooth Grin."

Dr. Seuss's feline protagonist may be "a cheerful, exotic and exuberant form of chaos," as the book's jacket copy asserts. But look at the children's faces watching the cat. They are not necessarily smiling. Their eyes resemble tunnels. *Oh, oh, oh*, they mouth as the cat balances the books and the tray and the cake and the boat and the fish in the bowl and the milk and the cup all on one foot hopping on the ball with its stripe round the middle. Now the rake and the red fan and the wooden toy man. Only the fan seems secured by the cat's tail, shaped like a cup hook. "But that is not all! / Oh no. / That is not all . . . ," as the action accelerates. Little wonder Sally's red hair bow quivers with anxiety as she grabs her brother's arm and they both plant their feet like croquet wickets.

Down comes the cake, and the frosting slaps over the plate, and the milk spills (but the bottle did not break!), and the rake's bent, and the boat looks like it's sailing on a wave of butter and cream. Down come the glass and the fan and the book splayed like a tent, and down comes the fish, oh the fish, tossed out of its fishbowl into a teapot, as a matter of fact, where he frowns, one fin in the air, "'Now look what you did!' / Said the fish to the cat. / 'Now look at this house!'"

Betty, cashier at the Rite Aid, had a steep beak with reading glasses perched at the very tip–classic Woolworth's fifties–wiry black hair, and veiny hands. Never satisfied with a simple financial transaction, she took mental notes. Whose wallet was stuffed with crisp twenties or pilled singles. Whose child pilfered a Baby Ruth and was he punished adequately? She sold booze to men, women, street people, rich people, and kept count, as if bottles were Weight Watchers points. Not much of a task for her memory the professor who purchased his daily fifth, sometimes missing a day if he sprung for a gallon. Her tongue clicked and slid over her teeth. "Is that *all* for you?" she asked. No response. "Sir? That'll be $13.53."

Years of this, she figured out which lady was the wife–the brusque, all-business one who didn't seem to care for conversation, who checked her change and left without a thank you. "Sweetie, you know I see your husband in here nearly every day getting him a fifth of that whiskey over there." Caught up short, I sputtered under my breath: "Whatever." Thinking: Nosey parker. Just do your job, please, and shut up. We're doing fine. He contemplates the big picture, I do the details. I *like* details. Flight arrangements, bills, doctors and dentists, chimney sweeping, furnace repair, taxes, ditching the sour milk and moldy bread. All the right moves we made in our lives—the babies, our relocation to the coast where he juggled a part-time teaching job, job search, book project, toddlers so I could have some writing time too, all without family around—those were his ideas. I did the packing. Didn't mind, couldn't imagine passing that job over to him. Commotion of glasses mixed with silverware, everyone's unfolded clothes thrown into the same suitcase or two. Who could live with that?

The science of fermentation is known as zymology. French chemist Louis Pasteur was the first known zymologist, when in 1854 he connected yeast to fermentation. Studying the fermentation of sugar to alcohol by yeast, Pasteur concluded that the fermentation was catalyzed by a vital force, called "ferments," within the yeast cells. The ferments were thought to function only within living organisms. "Alcoholic fermentation is an act correlated with the life and organization of the yeast cells, not with the death or putrefaction of the cells," he wrote.

Q: My husband has a sweet body odor after even one drink. I have a good nose and can always tell. Mornings, the bedroom smells syrupy, like peaches soaked in brandy. The odor has soaked into the pillows, sheets, even my own nightgown if he holds me at night. I can hardly sleep. I used to shower every other day. Now, it's every single morning. He's a teacher and I'm worried one of his students will notice too and he'll lose his job.

A: *The smell comes from ketones. In alcoholic ketoacidosis, alcohol causes dehydration and blocks the first step of gluconeogenesis. The body is unable to synthesize enough glucose to meet its needs, thus creating an energy crisis resulting in fatty-acid metabolism and ketone body formation. It happens in diabetes too. Is your husband Asian, by any chance? They often lack a certain enzyme, causing booze to be metabolized differently (and making them feel as if they are taking Antabuse).*

In any case, I suggest your husband visit a doctor.

The cat is back, bearing on his back an enormous box like a redwood Jacuzzi. He flips the hook and two blue-haired spawn rush out dressed in miniature full-body sleeper suits. But no, they aren't sleeping; they are *flying*, followed by contrails and rapid ink-slashes. They pause briefly to shake hands with poor Sally and her brother, then like gunshot dash off again. Thing One and Thing Two like to fly kites! High, higher, highest! In the house! No matter the spillage and untidiness! In comes mother's polka-dotted dress on a string. Down goes momma's vanity, perfume, and brush. Sally is blown off her feet. Brother grips a doorjamb for dear life, as two Things careen around corners, tear up the stairs. This is worse than any argument or fender bender. Says the fish, "No! No! / Those things should not be / In this house! Make them go!"

The kids knew he liked his ice chipped from the fridge door and a French jelly glass set to the right of his special chair. He had them well trained by age five; snack of Smokehouse almonds before dinner, or Goldfish in a salad bowl. He was their hero as he sat and sat and sat with his laptop, building mountains of cool stuff from eBay–antique fountain pens, Bakelite, letterpress furniture, or custom-made knives. Two dozen Catalin poker chips, spilling over the coffee table and onto the floor! Packages of fonts so heavy the postman wondered out loud if they weren't bars of gold. The knives were impressive, made of rippled steel, inlaid pearl on the grip, and blue-black blades. He called the girls to his chair, snapped his wrist forward to show them the cutting edge etched with curlicues. Again and again, he flipped the knife open. With each click he growled like a wolf and the startled children jumped back.

I stood before them, straining like the fish from its fishbowl: "Stop, please. Put that away. What are you, Crocodile Dundee or something?"

Who loves the fish? Prickly finned, frowning with wrinkled pink fishy skin. Each word overpronounced, clipped. No-fun fish, too strict, and always worrying about homework or junk food. Too easy to mock, lots of fun to run from with a snicker and hoot.

Shaving one morning, my husband lingered outside the girls' bedroom. Their noses were pressed to the back window, which was large and framed their small bodies with room to spare. In each hand they held a pastel-colored My Little Pony, and there were more on the floor behind them, piled in a heap. They paused in their play to stare down into the alley, a stone's throw from the house. On the asphalt, a drunk lay face down, his jacket oily, pants crumpled, and one of his shoes missing. He resembled a filled-in version of a police outline at a murder scene, right hand and knee raised, cheek turned to the left.

Drivers backed up, honking, then inched forward, negotiating their vehicles around him, but no one stopped or called. The man had a head of thick, black, only slightly disheveled hair, which unsettled Laura. "That looks like Dad," she said, turning to her sister. "Make that cat go away!" said the fish. "Tell that Cat in the Hat / You do NOT want to play."

Once I took a walk with my father, in town for just a few days. Showing obvious restraint, weaving the question around and about, he finally asked me if I thought my husband had a drinking problem. "Well no," I said, "he can handle a lot. Hardly ever gets drunk. He's a big guy." This I reported with only an ounce of concern, "Right, honey?"

Later, a famous poet came to visit, widow of a fiction writer well known for his addictions. She had thick hennaed hair and a maternal touch, waiting all day till they were alone before she took him out to the back porch: "Maybe you ought to shorten up on the booze, friend."

Spirit signals, like buoys blinking in high sun. In the moment they seemed irrelevant, unconvincing. But, peering out from the dark descended, their swaying lights formed a neat line straight to the shore. *I should have paid attention.* But he did pay attention in a backdoor way. Their warnings slipped in and smoldered along with his own low-register fear.

The mind grows languid that has no excesses.
—FRANCIS BACON

The sun spreads in the west like Courvoisier with a lick of blue flame. Excess, ecstasy. A going out, beyond, loss of possessions, self-possession, *excedere, excessum.*

> *Temperance is like wholesome cold, it collects*
> *and braces the powers of the mind.*
> —FRANCIS BACON

Patient, calm, sedate. *Abstinere.* I abstain, keep, hold. Where does *your* mind work best?

Like so many other writers, he suspected drinking was fuel for creativity. There was the evidence: books published, plays produced, grants won. Hemingway, Fitzgerald, Faulkner, James Wright. Still, he noticed the lapses, skin blotchy and cold; nerves when he gave a poetry reading or presented the same old material to his class as if he didn't know how. Once, a Target clerk called the only number she could locate in a stack of poetry portfolios left by the register. The student drove by to pick them up that afternoon and brought them to class. "Hey, absent-minded professor. Look what I found." They all had a good laugh. Ha! Ha!

Sally's bow droops like rain-heavy pansy petals. Mother's dress has been dragged across the carpet, spotted with lint, cat hair, cake crumbs. Brother holds an upside-down kite, and the fish issues commands from its teapot. What to do with a mess this wide and deep and tall? Every object has fallen cockeyed: frame on a wire, telephone off its cradle, crooked plates in a crooked pile, vase toppled, pink chair on its side kicking its fat little legs. This is some kind of hairbrushbowlsoapdishteacupbook soup! Where to start, where to start, if that is at all possible? "This mess is so big and so deep and so tall, we cannot pick it up. There is no way at all!" The children's arms hang like loose rubber bands; they're up to their middles in crap.

Lindsey B. Zachary points out in "Formalist and Archetypal Interpretations of *The Cat in the Hat*" that nearly half of the book's sentences end in exclamation points. There are several ways to voice this form of punctuation: One, with an excited lift like the cat's "Look at me! / Look at me now!" Two, with a scolding, insistent tone, as the fish declares, "He has gone away. Yes. / But your mother will come. / She will find this big mess!" To add heft Seuss uses caps: "Now what SHOULD we do?"

Zachary continues, examining the book through Northrop Frye's mythos of satire: "Throughout *The Cat in the Hat* there is . . . a comic struggle between two domains, one emphasizing traditional morals while the other is a fantastical explosion of chaos and entertainment." No wonder teachers and parents were worried the book would displace the staid and incredibly boring primer *Dick and Jane*. Imagine a classroom turned upside-down by the suggestion of FUN, not to mention AUTHORITY teetering on the slippery handle of a crooked umbrella!

Children love to be brought to the edge but rely on adults to be pulled back to safety. As Zachary notes, Sally and her brother "are watching the comic struggle between the worlds of order and fantasy, and they maintain their balance in the midst of the chaos simply by staying silent, eyes open." The fish does the talking, and like the fish, I tried to arrest the cascade of events set into motion by someone else's out-of-bounds behavior. Planted my body before him, pointed with my index finger, declared what he should or should not do. Control (or the attempt to control) was my disease, and it encompassed things large (drinking) and small (pillowcase folded just so).

But the cat had stolen the scene with his spit-takes, shaving-cream cakes, and over-the-top pranks. I was knocked aside, stiff and irrelevant. This is the lesson for Sally and her brother: no fish rules forever and a fish can look like a fool strung up on a kite string pulled through the house by Thing One and Thing Two. My sputtering speech, command, or inflexible view made no impression whatsoever.

When an alcoholic takes a drink, the alcohol affects his brain as a depressant, decreasing the activity of the nervous system. In order to keep the brain functioning normally, the brain attempts to chemically counteract and disrupt alcohol's action.

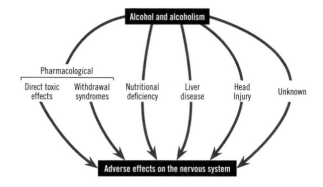

In simple terms, it ramps things up. Over time, more drinking is necessary to produce that confident, soothing effect.

One tequila, two tequila, three tequila, floor. When the alcoholic abruptly stops drinking, his nervous system suffers from uncontrolled synapse firing. Symptoms include anxiety, seizures, hallucinations, the "shakes," and even heart failure. The otherwise healthy individual has a significant risk of dying from withdrawal, if not properly managed. Hospitals and treatment centers use various pharmaceutical medications including barbiturates, clonidine, and vitamins like folic acid and thiamine to get the drunk through this early stage, which lasts roughly a few days. Then they work on his emotional, social, and spiritual recovery.

The staff at Hazelden knew he was a professor. So the first night they handed him a big stack of recovery books and asked him to prepare for a meeting the next day. Twelve, thirteen different titles, none of them difficult. He read the first one all the way through, took notes. The second, third, fourth. After that he skimmed: same message, well written or not. He had substantial recall. Even doped up with Librium, he was ready to quote, criticize the simplistic sentence structure, extol the points he agreed with. He could pass the test, no sweat. Next morning, seating himself in the counselor's office, he crossed his legs and leaned back, confident.

"Oh, we don't want a report. We thought we'd just get that out of the way. Now you can go on in there and join the group."

What followed was a militaristic routine endured because it helped get him through the day. The bed tight-sheeted, early breakfast in the stainless-steel cafeteria, AA meetings, steps, slogans, the psychologist half his age forcing a role-play opposite another drunk on his knees making amends. An arrogant PhD, his closest peer in the group (he thought), stormed off,

"I've got this, thanks, I'm good." No one tried to stop him. Though my husband chose this facility because it was close to the beach, the beach was not on the agenda. For a month he couldn't phone his wife, kids, even his father, who had been sober two years. Everything timed, scheduled, ten minutes for a shower, fifteen for dessert in the spotlight of the mess hall. Dessert! If he couldn't have a drink, he could still have his sugar straight like a cloud on the tongue. Oh, angel-food cake with cream-cheese frosting! Oh, chocolate meringue pie!

Chastened, the cat returns in his cat-driven, cat-manufactured, quickerpickerupper jalopy. It's a Rube Goldberg contraption with cockeyed springs and telescoping arms, none of them entirely solid or securely attached. But they do the job *Voom!* with a flourish and a pat. Even the hat is a little perkier on the cat's head as he maneuvers the controls and picks up the cake, rake, gown, milk, strings, books, dish, fan, cup, ship, and of course the fish, who sails into his fishbowl with a springy tail flip. Look at the children's faces! For once they are smiling, brows high, eyes bright. On his way out, the cat salutes and the fish relaxes just as Mother places the toe of a neat high-heeled shoe on the doormat. She looks composed too, the gentle drape of her coat, the S-curve of her calf, her slender hand lifted, "Hello."

There are diseases that die with a flourish and a *fffttt*. The course of medication is complete, the offending organ surgically removed–the story's over. Chronic disease, from the

Greek *khronikos*, "of time," is a never-ending tale no one wants to hear about. Arthritis, diabetes, high blood pressure. In the case of alcoholism, the end is "recovery," but more accurately, it's "disease control." The alcoholic must live in real time, stick to the program, keep up his meetings, slogans, steps, and *not drink*. Ever. Various studies show that anywhere from 54 to 90 percent of alcoholics are likely to experience at least one relapse, and two-thirds of these are within the first ninety days.

Social adjustment is a key factor in relapse prevention. Alcohol dependence froze this drinker's emotional and social skills at the age it began, around twenty-eight. Now he faced ordinary unpleasant experiences like colds, car accidents, kids who refused to do their homework, claustrophobic plane travel, a pissed-off wife, all without a buffer. I was recovering too, trying to extricate myself from, as the cliché goes, a *family* disease. This meant giving up control over a multitude of things (especially the alcoholic), disappearing on Tuesday and Thursday evenings for my own meetings with their focus on detachment and healing, phrases like "I'm sorry you feel that way" and "Let it begin with me." Both AA and Al-Anon have been called "selfish" programs, implying not the pejorative–self-centeredness to the detriment of others–but the idea that recovery must come first or we are of no value to anyone, even ourselves.

He was not a happy camper. Consider the cat without his hat, sack of tricks, Thing One and Thing Two, all his partners in crime. He did not bound through the door, feeling great, upending this and that with his bedraggled, swishy tail. His temper was short. He sat in his chair like a stone, afraid to move. And the girls steered clear. Even our Friday steak dinner at Jack

Fry's was dangerous because less than a month ago, it was preceded by a Seagram's and followed by a Courvoisier. Perrier on ice just didn't DO. Cranberry juice mixed with soda and lemon was NOT a perfect substitute.

It was more than a year before his nerves healed and he began to feel human again. A new wave of students joined the ranks of his admirers and the ones who had noticed his drinking moved on and never looked back. Another year at least till his humor returned and he was easier with all of us. The games continued, within reason. I noticed how deftly they were tailored to the girls' advancing ages, colored with a streak of sadness. "Listen to your mom," he said more than once. "Let's talk it over with Mom." But the dreams: a river floating hundreds of beer bottles, a bartender with his hand stretched out, "Double Aspen with a twist?" They kept on.

Open the sequel.

Page one shows a big room with sloping pink walls and a wide red floor. Happy home, everything neat. In the corner is a single white-curtained window, the glass lightly streaked. Peace and qui— . . . but wait, could it be? Outside, surrounded by sky, is the *cat*, peering in. Oh, say it's not so. Oh, stay away at least for today. His hat tilted like a road-construction barrel. His bowtie at attention. He twiddles his thumbs with a self-satisfied grin. He doesn't care what you're planning for lunch, or this promise or that. He's high as a kite, that cat. Raring to go and ready for FUN.

P E R *f* E C T
Tea

Highly suitable for someone
or something; exactly right.

Last night was a good time. Now stumble to the kitchen. Fish the spotted mug from the dishwasher, the one from Italy, favored for its height, white crackle glaze, and slender lip. Its footprint is small, mouth wide. No need to pinch the handle or fling out a naughty pinky; all four fingers fit.

Honey squeezed from the bear before milk, water, even tea. Then two inches of milk, usually skim, though whole milk is hardly a crime on Sunday. Cold water up to the rim and a scuffle for the right tea in a drawer with too many herbal numbers. Twinings Irish Breakfast. In Ireland, "tea" simply, enjoyed throughout the day and evening.

The microwave is fine. Two minutes forty-five seconds on high and the perfect mottled scrim rises to the top, the bag floating in a paisley of light milk-chocolate brown. No puffing, gasping cappuccino din. No inch-high foam all empty promise and mustache making. This cup is for immediate, wholesome, essential tea drinking. The buzz begins within four or five sips. Lucky day! I've got the *New York Times* and the font's not so tiny after all. I'm up for more than Arts and Leisure. A story on deep-space imaging, the cacao's genetic map, or why we're smashing protons together in the Large Hadron Collider. . . .

Monday morning: two bags.

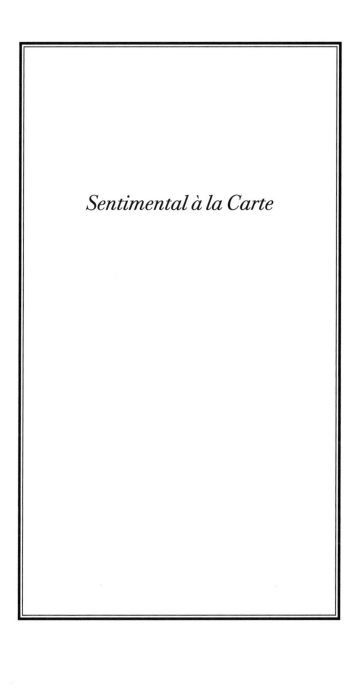

Sentimental à la Carte

Today's Specials:
Matzo brei fried in schmaltz
Wonton soup
Bea's Ho-made cherry pie
Kentucky bison filet
Steak tartare

Before their dough could rise, exiled Israelites fled Egypt, and thus we have matzo, poor man's bread, a reminder to be humble and not to forget what life was like in servitude. Eating it provokes a bitter sweetness. Chewing (with thought and dignity) offers both a lesson in humility and an appreciation of one's sense of freedom.

Salt, fat, and the bread of affliction. A tradition lost on four braided girls in their Monkees pajamas, sitting restlessly at the dining room table. Sunday morning Father rose early and pattered down to the kitchen dressed in his maroon-and-navy madras bathrobe. He laid out a large cast-iron skillet, sometimes butter, a little schmaltz (chicken fat), eggs, milk, and matzo in its bright orange-and-green Passover box. He broke up the hard, flat crackers, dipped them first in milk then egg, set the fat sizzling and laid the matzo down to fry. It softened, he salted, slid the pieces onto four plastic breakfast plates. Matzo brei was heaven, not hardship, when soaked with Aunt Jemima's syrup.

The expression "falling into the schmaltz pot" refers to plain old blind luck, like being born into a good family. Anyone this lucky is called "a schmaltz." How lucky we were to have a father, less distant than the standard fifties' and sixties' models, who taught the overhand crawl, bicycle riding, who drank socially but not excessively, who earned a stable living in upper-level U.S. government. For my thirteenth birthday, this MIT- and Stanford-educated "whiz kid" economist gave me a biography of Madame Curie. For my seventeenth it was Edward O. Wilson's *The Insect Societies*, with its glowing yellow cover and enlarged ant. Both gifts flattered my intelligence, implying I might share in his interests. They were books I carried with me everywhere like honorary degrees.

In the mid-1930s, schmaltz developed a pejorative sense, evoking excessive sentimentalism. The alternate usage is no doubt a reference to the fat itself–duck, chicken, or goose– overly rich, sickening. To the serious-minded, schmaltz is the kiss of death and can be applied in thick layers to art, music, literature, film, painting, conversation, interior decoration, and so on.

Most of us are sentimentalists about something; what provokes it can vary from decor to idea, from old-fashioned jukeboxes to *Das Kapital*. We give in to emotion till it clouds what we are actually seeing, hearing, or smelling. The scent of an apple pie (even if it's baked by Kroger) will provoke happy sadness; a tearjerker film will lead us to, well, tears. Everyone is subject. If the conditions are right, even the high-minded will allow a trickle of schmaltz to seep in.

Every night except Sunday, the Imperial Palace at Holiday Manor Mall features China Joe the piano player on a shiny black-lacquered baby grand, which sits at the center of a large dining area. The aquarium is full of carp and viscous water, the rug is sticky, and maroon napkins are annoyingly nonabsorbent. We ask for a balcony table with a bird's-eye view. Drinks appear in little amber glasses, and chopsticks are the cheap kind, fused together, splintery when broken apart. Jeffrey requests the steak and broccoli and I always ask for wonton soup with extra julienned vegetables, though the waiter sometimes defers: "No special orders." Finally, Joe slinks in, wearing a tuxedo and tossing his glossy black hair. The tip jar is an enormous brandy snifter where two one-dollar bills and a few coins puddle. He begins playing with a shrug.

"Climb Every Mountain" opens with a stiff, instructional tone. Moments later, Joe ascends with flourishes in the right hand. Soon he's leaning forward, full weight thrown against the keys as he reaches the steep rise to the refrain. He arrives with an enormous crescendo, rocking back and forth, full pedal on the big chords, his bangs now falling into his eyes. "Till you find yoooouuuurrr . . ." he pauses there, face down for a beat, and finally, "dreams" molto, molto tremolo.

Polite applause. "The Wind beneath My Wings" and "People" follow. I've never heard him touch the Golden Age standards–"They Can't Take That Away from Me," "It's Only a Paper Moon," "Dancing on the Ceiling," or "Mood Indigo," many with a dose of vinegar splashed in with the sugar. His preference? The owner's?

———

Here's Joe, launching into my favorite:

> Tale as old as time
> True as it can be
> Barely even friends
> Then somebody bends
> Unexpectedly
> Just a little change
> Small to say the least
> Both a little scared
> Neither one prepared
> Beauty and the Beast

In the air, bottle-green sprites, wisps of periwinkle, gold, and pink swirl above the piano like a whirlpool or gentle tornado. As if on cue, they uncoil and race throughout the restaurant, wrapping about the diners, warming, drawing them away from the particulars of their meal, company, day. There is a fraction of involuntary silence and hands hover in midair above plates and wine glasses, skin tingling, lifted by a thousand hairs. Inside voices hush, withholding the *darling you are deluded*. There will be wedding bells and gold necklaces, castles and longed-after champion horses.

If a song were edible, "Beauty and the Beast" would taste like Pop Rocks, candy rumored to make your stomach explode. China Joe knows exactly what he is doing; his is one of the few professions where sentimentalism might be specified in the job description. But I'm momentarily and deliciously unaware as he winds up the song with right-hand arpeggios, another pause and tossed-back hair. Dramatically, his hands drop off the keyboard to his side. I am the only one to applaud.

———

My soup arrives in a clever, egg-shaped bowl. Glorified chicken noodle with not nearly enough julienned vegetables.

It's OK. Just.

More sweet than savory. Saccharine tone, sappy movie, sugar-coated proposal, syrupy smiles, treacly get-well cards, and a *mwah* air kiss–all empty calories.

There *are* times when sweet will make you cry. I'm speaking of Bea's "Ho-made" cherry pie in Gills Rock, Door County. The area offers a mixed bag of delicacies. Cherries in all forms–fresh-picked from trees, freeze-dried, canned, frozen, or baked into scones and Danishes. Beer from Milwaukee, cheese curds, bratwurst, and traditional fish boils, where restaurant diners gather round a huge bubbling pot of whitefish, onions, and potatoes. Captain Jack throws gas on the open fire, flames leap, and suddenly, water boils over in a *whoosh*, taking with it any impurities. We line up with partitioned plates for our coleslaw, bread, and big hunk of fish doused with butter.

A slice of Bea's cherry pie is included in the deal. Mind you, this pie will not appear in the pages of *Bon Appétit*. The filling's canned, the crust merely acceptable and slapped on unceremoniously. Bea sprinkles granulated sugar to make it fancy, but the real blessing is ice cream, which blurs the whole thing into soup. Some days I'm willing to drive forty-five minutes down the twisty, evergreen-lined back roads for the pleasure, well worth it to no one but me. This is the pie I inhaled as a kid, pie I remember before slow food and artisan pizza, pie my parents used as prize for good behavior.

Nostalgia, like sentimentalism, suffers from a lack of rigor. Stops short at warm and fun. "Render the world, see it, and report it without loss, without perversion," said critic Mark Van Doren. Aim for economy, precision, clarity.

In the boutique restaurant, above the open grill, hang three white plaster goats. They are life-size, disconcertingly lifelike, attached by actual nooses tight around their necks. Death has drained them of color but not texture. Their heads tilt to the side; Xs over eyelids. Their bellies bulge. The menu features bison, beef, rabbit, quail. The artist is a member of PETA. Or not. The most obvious suggestion stands: Animals are objects; we kill them for our clothes, experiments, food. *They taste good.*

The sculpture is an experiment; the owners favor art that forces us to "reflect." They recognize that postmodernism with its sense of contradiction, indeterminism, and lack of sentimentality is hip. The delight we feel as soon as we fork a juicy bite of medium-rare grass-fed buffalo, locally grown; the twinge that follows, looking up from our plates at the goats, ghostly and corporeal. It's a risky way to decorate, particularly in a restaurant. Guilt is not a sentiment conducive to gustatory pleasure. But better this than teddy bears, ducks with bonnets, and fake fireplaces stirring up the good old days.

How do we separate *sentiment*–mere feeling and thus acceptable–and *sentimental*, with its exaggerated, misplaced emotion? "Sentiment is when a driver swerves out of the way to avoid hitting a rabbit on the road," wrote Frank Herbert. "Being sentimental is when the same driver, swerving away from the rabbit, hits a pedestrian." The driver in the first instance commits no crime. In the second, he demonstrates a grotesque moral hierarchy. Rabbit trumps human. Sentimental reveals its darker side.

David Barbarash and Darren Thurston of ALF (Animal Liberation Front) were charged in Vancouver with sending letters filled with razor blades to twenty-two hunting-trip guides. One executive received a letter saying, "You have been targeted for terrorist attack." Members of ELF (Earth Liberation Front) burned down a Vail ski resort, including seven separate fires, causing $12 million in damages. In their communiqué, they announced, "putting profits ahead of Colorado's wildlife will not be tolerated. . . . We will be back if this greedy corporation continues to trespass into wild and unroaded [sic] areas." Ecoterrorists are rough-edged sentimentalists: poor little animals, terrible people! People, who decimate rain forests, slaughter chickens and cows, burn holes in the atmosphere. We'd be better off without them, an earth overrun with innocent furry creatures. And, of course, members of PETA.

I was eleven when I had my first taste of raw beef. Observant Jews will only eat beef killed by a *shochet*, or "ritual slaughterer," then drained of blood, soaked in water, salted, washed, and cooked. But my Jewish father was not observant. He chopped the tenderloin himself, feeding it into an old-fashioned hand-cranked meat grinder, seasoned it with salt and pepper, stirred in egg yolk, capers, parsley, and minced onion. He singled me out for this delicacy, an unspoken affection. No sloppy kisses or bear hugs; my father had a fundamental distrust of sentimentality. Instead, I watched while he prepared the beef in our small kitchen, then we snuck out to the backyard and sat on the patio with one plate and two forks. Just the meat itself, no crackers or bread. No siblings crowding in or mother clucking her tongue. Just Sarah and Dad. It was better than a birthday. Sunny and cool. The meat was delicious.

Ever the educator, my father spoke its proper name–steak tartare, which, according to one legend, was first prepared by Mongols, who placed slabs of meat beneath their saddles to tenderize it before eating. On the run, of course. Dad left it at that but later confessed the real source was a condiment–tartar sauce–served alongside. Early chroniclers had misunderstood: That Mongol meat was intended to ease a horse's saddle sores. Thoroughly saturated with horse sweat, it would have been completely inedible.

The dish now appears in numerous countries, including Nepal, France, Slovenia, Poland, and Germany, where it's known as *Mett*, "ground raw pork without bacon." It is commonly served on slices of bread or small rolls called *Brötchen*. In the seventies, German restaurants spread their buffets with *Zwiebelmett*, in the shape of hedgehogs, decorated with onion quills and olives for eyes.

How adorable! And possibly stomach-turning, though strict local controls insist only the freshest pork is used, sold the day the pig is butchered. By law the fat content must be less than 35 percent, which is high enough, but as everyone knows it's the fat that makes it taste so good. Like a schmear of schmaltz on unleavened bread. Or oily chicken broth with dumplings.

What if we remove Joe the piano player and his rapt audience. Scratch the entire family enjoying a northern clime for ten elongated days. Eliminate sculptor, artist, conflicted diners, and ecoterrorists too. Let's make this a dry, uncontaminated story, *ohne Gefühl*. A fact-based account recited by Spock, a Vulcan who couldn't fathom human action motivated by emotion. Eat your baby? Illogical, and patently harmful to the baby.

Let's go further. Disengage my father from Judaism, Judaism from love, love from food, food from loss and longing. We could try an essay from the point of view of the mixing bowl or salt and pepper shakers or a pair of long fluorescent bulbs buzzing on the kitchen ceiling. Tame our instinct to anthropomorphize with a scientific inquiry into natural versus artificial light and its impact on the preservation of meat. Thermometer and microscope required to track the development of bacteria. Describe the consumption of unleavened bread, broken down into carbohydrates/sugars by amylase, the digestive enzyme found in your mouth, churned by your teeth into a bolus, when it's ready to swallow.

Let the data speak for itself.

It could be done. You first.

PER*f*ECT
Conversation

That which has attained its purpose.

"I love you."
"I love you too."

The Shape of Fear

She squatted against an outside brick wall, sweating on an unseasonably cool day. Camp was still in session, but her task this morning was protecting her belly, pressing her arms against it, trying to create a counterache that would distract her from the real ache. She mumbled, climbed into my car. Her whole body mumbled, a definite blip on the taciturn scale. "Have you had anything strange to eat?"

There was a nasty bug running around so I took her home.

Saltines with jelly, toast with margarine, and plain old Melba Rounds–all tossed into the garbage. I unwrapped her favorite processed cheese, sliced it into strips. Bought flexible straws and a bright green plastic cup and filled it with ginger ale. Stood with arms folded begging, finally raised my voice, "You must drink. You cannot go three days without drinking."

Girl took a little sip. OK?

Later at the hospital, a physician breezed into the examining room, unfolded her on the table as if she were a dinner napkin. He leaned on the child's abdomen, then released with exaggeration. It's called "rebound tenderness," sharp pain with the let-up of pressure, rather than application. Sign of trouble in the appendix. He checked off his mental list. Deep palpation over the descending colon, in the right lower quadrant of the abdomen. Rovsing's sign? His movements were inorganic, rote. Turned the patient on her side with right hip flexed to determine presence of psoas sign. Negative. Ditto the obturator sign; no pain in the hypogastrium. The girl was definitely sick but unfazed in any specific way by specific prodding.

"Not surgical," his conclusion, "probably just flu. You can go home now."

That night I dreamed my child in a cup of milk. Looked down to see the milk rise up to her nose. Took a quick swallow to keep her from drowning.

It is a fine example of faience–a porcelain box with cabriole legs and ormolu fittings, hand-painted in the Romantic style. On the lid, a man embraces a woman, her bared breast a pink pastille, flowers flung aside now that they have got down to the heart of the matter. Underneath, someone has replicated the Meissen mark, implying that the box was fit for Augustus Rex, more likely his queen.

Technically a jewel casket; I made good use of it. Not for jewels, for I had none. Not for decoration at all, unless you call scraps of paper covered with anxious scribblings decorative.

But let me backtrack a bit. Before it came into my possession, the jewel casket was filled with great-grandmother's necklaces, bangles, a gold watch she intended to refinish. These were wrapped in white Kleenex so as not to chafe against each other. The box sat on her dresser, a nice piece itself of inlaid wood and brass pulls.

When she died, the casket was emptied of jewels in preparation for great-grandmother's ashes. Refined, beloved Marianne–matriarch of an enormous clan, fit to be buried in decorated porcelain lined with blue velvet. Until one cousin came to her senses. The box was ready to go, perched on a French writing desk in the front hallway. Family idling, coated and sad. One cousin turned to the other, saying, "What are we doing? Are we sure we want to bury this thing? It's over a hundred years old."

And thus the ashes were tipped into a FedEx envelope, later into a conventional urn, still later that morning buried properly with a scattering of Lutheran prayers, and for those who didn't believe, fidgety silence.

Again the ER. Again the girl was unfolded on the table, dressed in a gown covered with blue fish. Two more days–making five–without much sustenance and only thimblefuls of Kool-Aid.

This time we were simmering. We pleaded our case to the receptionist and still hung five hours for someone from surgery. The surgeon arrived, ducking in for a few minutes between her own patients. She proposed a pelvic and rectal exam to get a better look inside, deliberate probing for sensitivity. If the appendix lies entirely within the pelvis, there's often complete absence of abdominal rigidity, so her investigation was shamelessly thorough. I asked if my daughter might need privacy, turned abruptly to leave, only to have the surgeon grab my arm and order my return. "She needs her mother right now. Please."

But the patient was underresponsive, except to the indignity of it all. Or she was holding it in, holding out for a lesser diagnosis. I too edged into denial that anything more serious than flu was at hand. After all, that first doctor with the unpronounceable name, hadn't he confirmed it two days earlier? The flu. Could we go home now?

Another two-hour wait and finally, by ultrasound, the appendix was sighted, tucked behind her uterus. It was indeed ruptured, flailing like a snipped hose, spreading little pellets of excrement into her gut. The patient was whisked into surgery, promised she would be sleeping like she'd never slept before. There followed an uneventful forty-eight hours blessed by on-demand morphine and as many popsicles as she wanted. She was only thirteen. The other food she craved was French fries, which of course were verboten.

In 2006, a graphic designer from the United Kingdom named Orlagh O'Brien conducted a survey she called *Emotionally Vague*. The aim was to create a graphic or visual representation for each of five emotions: anger, joy, fear, sadness, and love. Two hundred and fifty men and women from over thirty-five countries between the ages of six and seventy-five responded. The sample was a mix of friends, their friends, colleagues, and strangers.

QI: *What makes you feel this emotion (let's say "fear")? Write it down.*

After articles and prepositions, abstractions topped the list: "being," "death," "alone," "heights," "people," "dark," "darkness," "control," and so on. O'Brien arranged them into a stack, a box of words, with the most common in black, fading down to the least common in light silver: "spaces," "unfamiliar," "past," "think," "war." Where were the specifics? The rusty nails, dysplastic cells, rotten eyeteeth, and wandering eyes? I half expected the list to work like a microscope, from general to particular, group to individual, but most of us, even the solitary fearful soul, never get beyond the broadest description. Language was a soft, floppy tool for this group trying hard to communicate what it felt. The result was like a fading Beckett monologue.

the of in being death alone—heights
people—when dark—darkness control—I
not—snakes—to a—and—future—illness—I'm
on at—loneliness—love—my bad—big—flying
loss—loved—night—violence—walking—wrong
about —dogs—don't—failure—falling—family
ghost—ghosts—it—lack—me—movies—ones—or
presentation—scarey—something—speaking
spiders—thing—thinking—time—unknown—what
able—aggression—aggressive—authority
earth—feel—feelings—gangs—groups—have
house—insects—is—knowing—life—losing—money
much—nervous—no—noise—out—past—public
sea—sharks—sleeping—snake—someone
spaces—street—suddenly—terrorism—tests
think—too—unfamiliar—war

Q2: *How do you feel this emotion in your body? Draw anything you wish.*

Hundreds of pen scratches were stacked, layered one over the other, the human shape with lines crossing and recrossing every inch of its body. Some strokes spill over the edges too, though they concentrate in several places: palms, radial arteries, and most obviously, the torso—a fat black smudge from lower abdomen to the tip of the skull. Fear lives in the body's core, taking up light residency in the extremities, where we experience that tingly feeling as an oncoming bus nearly sideswipes us standing at the curb.

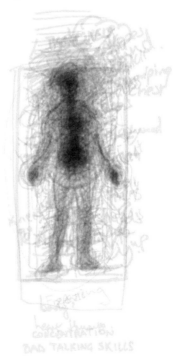

The on-call resident flipped back the sheet so he could observe her incision: a jagged eye shape below and to the right of her navel. It was time to remove the drain. The wound would stay open, heal from the inside to prevent infection, he explained, but first this catheter's got to come out. He planted himself at bedside, unclipped the waste bag, let it fall to the floor; then prodded around the outside of the incision with gloved fingers, hoping to force the tube out by itself. With each bit of pressure, the patient sucked in her breath and held. She was not a vocal child, but she was hurting.

A thin nylon cord snaked within the tube and this the doctor stretched, released, stretched, released, stretched, released. My daughter twisted right and left, angling for the ceiling or anywhere else but here. The resident's tug of war was past her bearing, but he scarcely looked up. He focused instead on her belly and his trouble unhitching the thing, as if he'd hooked a fish somewhere deep inside her abdomen and was now wrestling it into the air. She whimpered, "Can we call for someone else?" when finally the apparatus popped out with a spurt of bacteria-rich fluid.

A nurse muttered pessimistically, "Looks like secondary infection to me."

"Fear, jealousy, money, revenge, and protecting someone you love," said Max Halliday, listing the five important motives for murder. I was furious: *Whose fault would that be, all that stirring around in her wound by a novice, a novice who doesn't half know what he's doing, would you please get someone in here who does, this hurts, she's hurting, PLEASE?* I then chose this moment of all moments to slip away from the child, swing through the hallway, down the elevator, through the automatic doors over the blacktop and into my parked car. There I let loose a howl–cheeks drawn, mouth like a pie plate. My tongue dropped into the pocket of my lower jaw. The sound was coarse, unmusical, void of letter, syllable, or phrase. What else can I tell you except no one screams like this in the movies, it was too chest-deep and ragged. Inhalation, sigh, inhalation, then another animal wail into the sour air of our Toyota van. Fear, not surprisingly, makes you stink.

~~

Q3: *Where do you feel fear in your body? Draw one spot only.*

And now the emotion rises from the paper like a corpse from water. Just the forehead, nose, mouth, throat, and chest. Damp spots in the gut. We know the figure has arms and legs for the silver imprints where his hands, groin, thighs, and shins would be. But he has forgotten them. Fear looks like a mounted insect, or a skeleton without the small connecting bones. One envisions a body semiburied in mud, clay, or sand, the archaeologist patiently brushing.

Q5: *Does your fear have direction? If yes, draw arrows.*

Cue the giant made of arrows, hundreds of them, like a disorganized Celtic wicker man. Throw in a few twigs and broomsticks. His belly stuffed with whatever might be conceived as desirable or delicious to the gods: cattle, chickens, garlic, goats, criminals. Burn it, set the wicker man aflame as sacrifice. If you believe, it will put your mind at ease.

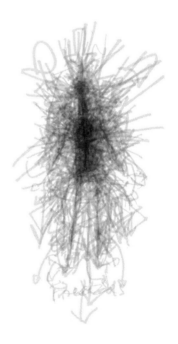

Quietly I wished for a bit more of my rightful inheritance and spoke of Marianne's promises. We were close, and the jewel casket reminded me of her reassuring cornflower-blue bedroom with its canopy bed and Chinese carpet. So the mothers and fathers and aunts and uncles suggested they ship it to Sarah. Upon my return from Wisconsin, the little casket was lying inside my front door wrapped in bubbles, duct tape, and a white cardboard carton delivered ground-to-ground by FedEx.

I named it the God Box and, right here and now, apologize if I must for the born-again, Hallelujah touch. A no-nonsense friend suggested this reasonable alternative to praying, which at the time I didn't really care for: Write it down on a note card. Drop it in the box and let God handle it. Repeat as necessary. Don't worry if you fill the thing up. Just keep stuffing it in there.

Curious, how anxiety matures over a lifetime—pure imagination at first, like masked men under the bed or giant lizards in the basement. Later some realism slips in—car accidents, airplane crashes—bicoastal flying possible only with fingers and legs crossed and palpitations at the very sign of turbulence. At forty, on folded index cards, in complete sentences, I scrawled my grown-up requests: *Keep my girls safe and healthy. Find me a job. Stop his drinking.* Later, as these fears recurred, I took to shorthand: *Jeff. Martha. Paycheck. X-ray.*

Psychologists hypothesize that fear motivates religious faith. For this dreamer—who willingly suspends disbelief in literature, even in bad movies, who toyed with the idea of an afterlife blanketed with clover and poppies, who saw the world as unlikely without a sentient, larger-than-the-world being– it helped. Sometimes for a minute, sometimes for a week. My anxiety, transferred to featherweight bits of crumpled cotton and water, sat apart from me, mingling for a time with the rest of the world's dander and dust. I felt oddly light and insignificant and that was good.

If you can listen objectively, the sound of fear is amplified tinnitus. Movies have caught on with their edgy violins. What would a murder be without that dissonant sawing? Eagles scream. Harpies, winged death spirits, scream. There is even a bird called the American Harpy Eagle named for the mythological bird with a woman's head. *Harpy* means "to snatch." Food. Fleeing creatures.

The earliest recorded use of the noun *scream* was in 1513. The sound appeared as soon as there was a mouth, any kind of mouth or beak or scaly slit. German artillery in flight in World War II made a terrifying noise and thus, the term *screaming meemies* came into existence to describe battle fatigue caused by exposure to enemy fire.

A scream is the prayer of an animal who cannot speak or write or draw or assume the posture of a saint.

My daughter's body torqued on the sheet like a butterfly pinned to white paper. Reason enough for a mother to shriek like a harpy.

Dear Mr. Cornell,

I hear you have fashioned a box, specifically, a wooden jewel casket lined with velvet, in honor of the great nineteenth-century ballerina Marie Taglioni. I heard you had a vision, seated in your kitchen next to the stove. Peering out the window, lifting your gaze to a nearby office building, you caught sight of her pirouetting across the top floor. You believed she was real. Did you call out to her? Wave with a handkerchief? Somehow I think not. If indeed she had danced across centuries and continents to appear before you, I think you were too shy, too frightened of notable women.

Instead, this spectacular jewel casket. Three rows of four glass cubes, each inserted into square indentations, each atop a base of blue "windows." And below that, ever so visible through the cubes: bits of sand, crystal, and rhinestones, all resting on a mirrored surface. May I say how much I love the blue label fastened to the inside of the lid? May I test your patience and transcribe it here?

On a moonlight night in the winter of 1835 the carriage of Marie Taglioni was halted by a Russian highwayman, and that enchanting creature [was] commanded to dance for this audience of one upon a panther's skin spread over the snow beneath the stars. From this actuality arose the legend that to keep alive the memory of this adventure so precious to her, Taglioni formed the habit of placing a piece of artificial ice in her jewel casket or dressing table where, melting among the sparkling stones, there was evoked a hint of the atmosphere of the starlit heavens over the ice-covered landscape.

Not an explanation, of course. You were sparing with those. *Frugal with money, retentive with meaning.*

I too have a jewel casket. It gives me great comfort. It's older and plainer than yours, dating to the mid-nineteenth century. Fashioned without Bacall, Sontag, Miranda, or Taglioni in mind. How poignant that your infatuations were never consummated. But how else would we have your boxes to treasure and appreciate? Would that all our coping mechanisms resulted in masterpieces!

An aside: Some say you were agoraphobic. Oh, fear can wreak havoc on a body. Remember when Helen caught sight of you outside Whitman's, doubled over, moaning on a bench in Madison Square Park? Dyspepsia, they called it, and didn't you suffer until that gentle, fellow salesman suggested Christian Science. You called it "the natural, wholesome, healing and beautiful thing." Prayer and devotion, an excellent way to ease anxiety, to hold bodily impulses in check. I wonder now if religion helped with your stomach pain. What do you think, Mr. Cornell? I'd be most curious to know.

With utmost respect and most sincerely yours,

During the days that followed, we saw a good deal of hand washing as nurses entered the room and when they left. But no special gowns or masks, and visitors weren't encouraged to follow any sanitary procedures at all, though I played with my daughter's hair, applied cold washcloths, and assisted with bathing. Orderlies dragged mops around, and the trash was emptied listlessly.

Methicillin-resistant *Staphylococcus aureus* or MRSA is a perilous variety of the common staph infection. It's prevalent among patients with open wounds, invasive devices (such as chest tubes or drains), and weakened immune systems. The press dubbed it the "superbug" when it was identified in 1961, but it's taken a long time for protective protocol to become standardized in hospitals. For three decades the bacteria was busily making its own rounds, setting up warm little colonies on elevator buttons, bathroom door handles, and cafeteria cutlery.

Today, medical staff wear sterile gowns, gloves, masks, and puffy disposable slippers. There's vigorous cleansing with special soap containers permanently affixed to the wall. MRSA-infected patients are isolated from the rest of the hospital community and large yellow warning signs are posted outside their rooms. All this just a little too late for a post-op thirteen-year-old girl with a gaping wound in her abdomen. Here, our precise follow-up instructions:

1. Lay out the wrapped saline flush syringe, alcohol wipe, IV cap, sanitizer, and IV bag.
2. Punch the IV bag with tubing, squeeze to release the air.
3. Sanitize hands, wipe down the PIC and IV portals with alcohol.
4. Remove the syringe cellophane, tap and push to release any air, screw it into the PIC line, and flush.
5. Unscrew the syringe, remove the IV tube cap, push the tube into the PIC line.
6. Release the flow of medicine from the bag and wait for an hour while the drug enters with a chill into the patient's body.

Vancomycin is one medicine of choice for MRSA, a powerful antibiotic commonly used in worst-case scenarios. A PIC line is threaded under the skin through a vein near the elbow to a larger vein in the chest. It stays in place for a month, or however long the treatment. Visiting nurses named Meredith and Tiffany came by the house at the start. They frightened the dogs but were understanding and quick. Their aim was to pass the job on to Dad or Mom or anyone with a stable hand.

Perhaps a step or two has been conflated, though my memory of IV protocol is mostly pristine. It was a kind of knotted safety rope through scary terrain. Certainly this is how soldiers, police, and firefighters contain their fear, bearing down on the small points, the physical routine of unpacking the hose, oiling the weapon, unscrewing the coupling counterclockwise and easing it back. Focus the eye and the mind, narrow it as if through a camera lens or binoculars. The mind avoids everything but this six-or-seven-step system, repeated once in the morning, again at night. It's even possible to abstract the body lying on the bed, together with its wincing. Though I often stroked my child's arm, it became just an arm or a wrist, anybody's arm or wrist, and I pretended not to love it.

In the year 433, St. Patrick prepared to confront and convert Lóegaire, high king of Ireland. He was aware an ambush lay ahead aiming to slaughter him and his group en route to the court. He wrote a prayer to strengthen himself with God's protection, not unlike St. Paul's exhortation to "put on the whole armor of God."

Christ be with me, Christ within me,
Christ behind me, Christ before me,
Christ beside me, Christ to win me,
Christ to comfort and restore me.
Christ beneath me, Christ above me,
Christ in quiet, Christ in danger,
Christ in hearts of all who love me,
Christ in mouth of friend and stranger.

During the march they sang the sacred song. As the druids lay in hiding, ready to kill, they saw not Patrick and his men, but a gentle doe followed by twenty fawns.

St. Patrick and his men were saved.

The prayer became known as The Deer's Cry, The Lorica, or St. Patrick's Breastplate. A lorica is an incantation spoken for protection. In addition to being recited by monks, loricas could also be found inscribed on the shields or armorial trappings of knights, who might whisper or sing them quietly before going into battle.

One way to dispel one's fears is to inscribe them on paper, hide them in a box, or imagine them sailing off on little boats into heaven or wherever God lives. The St. Patrick's Breastplate is different; it calls the protector down, into, and around the body like a blanket, a tent under the elements. We are singled out, safeguarded, beloved. I first chanted the Lorica on a flight to Atlanta while the plane pitched and groaned through a thunderstorm. Each line was another layer of safety, and I imagined them settling one by one until I was surrounded, warm and dry.

Because a spark small as a comma can blow a bridge off its foundation. Because fear like an ant will bear a whole mind away.

At first, skin heals the way a river dries up. The depths of the wound grow shallow and we are no longer afraid to look at the bottom with its mysterious eddies and darknesses. One can imagine poking a stick, but tenderly, tenderly, and feeling some immediate, reassuring resistance.

Then the edges begin to draw together, in slow-motion, a gradual knitting of one shore to the other. A raised and reddish scar is the final evidence of the river on a map. The water is gone, sunk down far beneath the riverbed. Then the scar too diminishes, drains of blood till it is a twist of quicksilver across the belly.

After her incision healed, the trauma disappeared from the girl's mind too. She remembered nothing about the drainage tube, bed, injections, and ache. A near-complete erasure that one can easily forgive. A kind of wisdom.

Not everyone forgets. Not Mother. I'll fly over this territory again and again. The fear for my daughter's life is now part of who I am, the suffering savored.

I dream of an observation deck above Niagara, close to the engorged, blue-black current before its fall, and fleetingly, think about falling. I could play dumb, dare myself. The temptation rings in my teeth, like ice chips, or a tuning fork pressed to the bone.

At ease, Mother.

P E R *f* E C T
Sleep

Free from any flaw or defect in condition; faultless.

I remember only one such sleep, following my firstborn's delivery by C-section. I was under the influence of morphine and a pure, thorough, body exhaustion. The first course was upward, a mix of things half-heard, only partially understood, and so wrapped in imaginative ribbon. The rattle of a blood cart became a tree with spoons in place of leaves. A nurse became a lifeguard with layers of zinc on her nose. Her announcement over the intercom, the answer to all those dream exams.

I say upward, because so much sleep is depicted as falling. Mine was not so. The room with all its detail receded, and I rose with a slight toiling up up up into the sun, to the second course, a kind of plateau. This was new land, very flat, very white, a salt field or desert made of chalk. Patches of dream flew against the sun–a miniskirt, some costume jewelry–but they didn't engross me. When I was hungry, I ate coconut. When thirsty, I drank the milk. This went on for hours, this perfect sleep.

I reached the end by backstroke, the mind carving shoulder blades and wings in the sand. I stroked and coasted, sculled and skidded. Soon I began to wake, down into the township, the atrium, the bed, then lower into a squalling sound. I found the baby's face in mine: *Oh, there you are.*

On Selfishness

Everything has either a price or a dignity.

—KANT

I did not have three thousand pairs of shoes.
I had one thousand and sixty.

—IMELDA MARCOS

Roger Hargreaves's storybook character Little Miss Selfish is green, shaped like a beehive. She wears yellow heels, blue gardening gloves, and a bright yellow hat tied with a blue and red ribbon. Her mouth is turned down in a snotty frown. Little Miss Selfish doesn't share. The only thing she ever thinks about is herself.

In the French version, she's a Mrs.—Madame Moi-Je. A double-thick me/I.

Always first in line for brunch, she helps herself to the buffet, sits down at the family table, polishes off her bacon and waffles, and leaves before anyone else is served. A blood sugar dive could be the instigator. In that case, she'd do anything to get her hands on a piece of bread, even pluck a half-eaten roll off someone's plate. The blood *demands* sustenance, beats against the brain till it secures quick satisfaction. Yes, there are plenty of medical excuses for bad behavior. During the trial for the murder of Harvey Milk, a psychiatrist testified that Dan White's diet of junk food exacerbated his depression and mood swings. Diminished capacity or, as it came to be known, the Twinkie Defense. Unfortunately, it's not just hunger that makes Miss Selfish butt in line. She's *always* first, hungry or not. Nothing like a crowd waiting to board a plane or vaporetto or ski lift to stimulate her sense of entitlement. Her behavior at a 50 percent off sale is atrocious, all elbows, tossing hangers and clothes everywhere. Furthermore, the correct way to play tennis is her way. The right call is hers. Her friends would be wise to follow her stage directions; otherwise they will make a bad play. Miss Selfish rules, without persuasion or sensitivity.

Two girls lollygag at the edge of a large pond. It's a hot, dusty evening and they are merely passing time, vaguely aware of each other. Coincidentally, they decide to throw a rock at exactly the same moment: kerplunk/kerplunk. The ripples spread in broad half-circles intersecting on their way to the center of the lake. Some die out; others bounce back, reverse direction toward the shore, where they appear as light wavelets, shooshing noises tickling the sand. The girls watch, fascinated. Abruptly one child snaps into action, combing the shore, scuttling about like a gull searching for meat. In fifteen minutes flat she has scooped up all the best rocks and filled her pockets. "Can we share?" She will not share. Each rock plops into the water with a satisfying boink, or if she's lucky, skims across the surface like a dragonfly before sinking unceremoniously. The other child appears deflated, arms at her side. Her adversary grows large and furious in her movements, a giant weed whacker, all spinning arms and splashing. She can feel the spray on her face, like spit, and steps away. She'll find something else to do.

The word *selfish* was coined by Presbyterians in the seventeenth century, according to Hacket's *Life of Archbishop Williams*. It's translated *égoïste* in French, *itsekkäiden* in Finnish, and *önérdekű* in Hungarian.

Ego. Itself. One.

British biological theorist Richard Dawkins adopted the word for his gene-centered book on evolution, titled *The Selfish Gene*. Dawkins claims that genes act as if they are self-centered and the purpose of evolution is the survival of the information in the genes of the individual. Over a long period of time, the genes passed on from generation to generation are ones serving their implicit self-interest (to continue being replicated). Dawkins's proponents argue that the gene, as unit of selection, usefully completes and extends Charles Darwin's theory of evolution, before basic genetics was understood.

On a lighter note, Ambrose Bierce defined selfish in his *Devil's Dictionary* as "devoid of consideration for the selfishness of others." Why do we laugh at this? Because we recognize immediately that it's true, a formula with selfishness on both sides of the equal sign.

Imagine a pristine and very expensive Mexican beach resort called "A," where every stray wrapper is scooped up instantly and a hand outstretched is filled with a glass of minted ice tea. The clientele is privileged, the sand is raked nightly, and the ocean glistens as if it too were minty and iced. Twenty feet away from the bright umbrellas and chaises a long thick rope runs from water to street, confining local vendors to their portion of the beach, an area known as "B," though legally it is all public beach. Crowded and hot, the vendors shift from one scalded foot to the other. Trinkets and shawls, sombreros and jugs. Striped, tightly woven table runners and bright parasols.

No one from A crosses over to B. No exchange of coin, greeting, or glance. From A's point of view, B doesn't exist. One of the privileged sun worshippers speaks outside her privilege to say that most privileged people she knows are what we might easily call selfish. They prefer not to associate with those outside their circle. They have security systems, privacy issues, bold borders around their privilege.

But in fact, this cordoning off, this box-making, is not only the habit of privilege. A three-year-old will listen for language that suits her needs. For example, Mother insists with the power-words *have to*. You *have to* go to bed now. You *have to* wear shoes outside. Mother's hands clutch her daughter's arms, steer her upstairs, guide her foot into the Velcroed sneaker. The child feels her body positioned according to Mother's wishes. Not forced exactly, but expertly manipulated. Interesting. The child tries the expression herself. She bets on *have to* because she knows the words have muscle. I *have to* drink honey in my milk. I *have to* eat a chocolate cupcake. I *have to* wear both shirts and my favorite dress. Gentle, civilized *please*s, *may I*s, *share*s float everywhere, but they do not strike the child as utile, not yet. Bit by bit, brick by brick, she is fencing off her portion of the beach. *Her* beach.

A selfish instinct has its root in our earliest ancestors, and all of us pass through a selfish stage. Left to her own devices, a three-year-old might steal a turkey sandwich from her sister, forage through the pantry, and eat nothing but Oreos and Cheez-Its. God forbid, she would pee wherever she felt like it, or even shove open the door and rush into the dangerous street. Luckily, this little girl has a refining influence in her parents, specifically, Mother of Headstrong Toddlers. Though there is no instruction book on how to live socially, Mother has experience, which she naturally imparts. If the child grabs her sister's Elmo doll or worse, snatches a cracker off a stranger's plate, her mother will set her straight with another little lecture about asking politely, sharing, and showing consideration for others. Eventually the child will get it and, thus, with a little less selfishness, her socialization begins. Chances are, she'll never thank her mother. As Freud noted, we never really forgive the person who civilizes us.

If, however, her selfishness persists beyond childhood, it will restrict her ability to empathize. She'll see less of the world, deny the value of other points of view and, at the very extreme, risk becoming morally stunted, or even criminal. At the very least, a kind of self-petrifaction might set in.

My notion of mountainous beauty was formed by two months in Switzerland's Hasliberg, with its Rosenlaui Glacier, Reichenbach Falls, and twelve-thousand-foot peaks. It took days to hike the Jungfrau, to even draw close—the Nordwand sheer and unassailable without advanced equipment and experience. On cloudy days, the glacier glowed blue with grayish parallelograms that gave the ice a houndstooth appearance. Wind off the backside of the mountains caught snow and tossed it sideways, a horse tail. Cloud layer followed and I knew to expect the infamous föhn—balmy wind rushing down the valley, turning snow into aquamarine meltwater.

Layer this image over the aged Shenandoahs, rolling gently upward from green-blanketed valleys in north central Virginia. Though these mountains are beautiful to others, I cannot abide their weak lines and soft silhouettes. They suggest a flaccid resistance to weather, a lack of character. I kick a bit of crumbled rock to demonstrate. Clay. Powder. The highest peak is a knob, just over four thousand feet. Hardly a mountain at all.

A selfish person enters a scene, any scene, with a constrained, preformed, self-centered focus.

The film *Being John Malkovich* illustrated an extreme version of this. Craig Schwartz, a forlorn filing clerk, discovers a strange portal behind a filing cabinet. When he enters, he slips down a long chute and suddenly finds himself inside the mind of the actor John Malkovich, experiencing everything that John sees, touches, and hears. Later, Malkovich himself enters the portal and also finds himself in the head of actor John Malkovich, a world where everyone looks like him and can say only "Malkovich." The setting is an elegant restaurant. There are white tablecloths and a large set of windows overlooking a harbor. Nearly every table is occupied, crowded with diners–young or old, stooped or spry, decked out or dressed casually–*all of them* bearing John Malkovich faces. It's a jarring sight to anyone who is not John Malkovich. Is it comforting to John? Nightmarish? Fifteen minutes later he is tossed out of his brain into a ditch somewhere near the New Jersey Turnpike.

Our species has evolved far beyond purely instinctual behavior, the only animal blessed (or cursed) with radical self-awareness. We invented the concept of selfishness and have the ability to choose between two options: experience the world as an extension of ourselves, or stand back and try to imagine it from another person's point of view. In a real restaurant, no one wears a John Malkovich mask to suit the egotistical vision of John Malkovich. But if a self-centered person walked in she might see only what she was in the mood to see: a pleasing nose or lip or Brooks Brothers suit, a plate of oily greens with pignoli and golden raisins. Suppose a waiter steps forward with a single red rose. He's just doing his job with that extra-special customer service touch, but she's thinking, "What can he possibly want? Does he not know I detest red roses?"

As for the rose, it's only selfish if it desires every
other flower in the world to be a rose.

—OSCAR WILDE

In my favorite restaurant there's a heavyset man who regularly dines at a window seat, ordering without fail a huge plate of French fries. He's a veterinary bone surgeon, but my eye passed over him with little consideration. He's overweight, and look how little he attends to his condition. French fries! Several months later, my basset hound tumbles down the kitchen stairs and I'm forced to bring the suffering animal to this very surgeon. I walk into the examining room, uncertain the man will have much to offer.

That is, until he begins to explain, while stroking the dog's tricolored fur, the process of repairing a shoulder that has been yanked from its socket. He points to an indistinct area on the X-ray, circling one finger over the afflicted joint, speaking in a crisp yet gentle instructional tone. I value intelligence, and the doctor's is considerable. He has calmed the animal with his touch. In my mind, his pounds of flesh melt away until all I can see is the hound's easy up and down breathing under the surgeon's hand. The doctor's mild demeanor acts like affection on my anxiety too and I fall into a state of hypnotic relaxation. He gently adjusts my suspicion, prejudice, impatience, and brushes them aside till I can't believe I once doubted him.

It takes terrific force to pry open the window in a selfish person's house. A motorcycle accident, anaphylactic shock after eating a strawberry, the fall of a beloved animal down a flight of very slippery stairs.

～

Un- is our most prolific English prefix. At its very core, it's a negation of everything that follows: untruth, undeniable, unheard of. The opposite of selfishness is unselfishness. Not selfish, not thinking first and foremost of one's self.

In *The Weight of Glory*, C. S. Lewis complained, "If you ask twenty good men today what they thought the highest of the virtues, nineteen of them would reply, 'unselfishness.' But if you had asked almost any of the great Christians of old, he would have replied, 'love.' You see what has happened? A negative term has been substituted for a positive." Doing good things for others is not enough; you must go without those good things yourself. Indeed, self-denial is a zenith, the highest virtue. Lewis blamed Stoicism, which teaches the development of self-control and fortitude as a means of overcoming anger, fear, jealousy, lust, and other damaging states of mind. The sage—a person who has attained moral and intellectual perfection—suppresses these emotions. As Marcus Aurelius, the first Stoic emperor of Rome, advised in his *Meditations*, "Be like the cliff against which the waves continually break, but which stands firm and tames the fury of the water around it." Deny yourself and you will live a good life. Death is a relief because it represents the end of desire and its attendant unhappiness.

It's not clear if Aurelius intended his writings to be published, but the diary, which he also called *To Himself*, provides an interesting snapshot of a would be Stoic sage at work. In it, he reminds himself of Stoic teachings, reproaching when he has fallen short: "The wise man sees in the misfortune of others what he should avoid." How close did Aurelius come to living a good life? A social reformer who helped the poor, slaves, and convicted criminals, he also was a fierce persecutor of early Christians. Press against one vein, another will inflate. He was, after all, emperor of Rome, responsible for safeguarding its borders.

The word *altruism* was popularized in 1830 by French philosopher Auguste Comte and is often presented as an alternative to *unselfishness*. Comte borrowed it from a legal phrase, *l'autrui*, or in full, *le bien, le droit d'autrui* "for the good, the right of others." A truism. All truisms, the tremendous number of *other* beings who pace the sidewalk after a rainy day, who eat cereal from the box, who happen upon a dead cat and spend the morning weeping. At the very least we must know they are there, significant for their existence, not for what they can or cannot do for us. The truly altruistic act out of a selfless concern for others. They get close, very close, close enough to see skin pores and saliva. They open all their senses like a barn door and let the information flow in. They forget their own skin and ticking pulse, anticipate when the other's need arises, and give at the right moment.

The truly altruistic even love others, though that love may not be as extraordinary as that of Mother Teresa, who said, "What we need is to love without getting tired." Teresa demonstrated her compassion by touching, wrapping her arms around castaways–lepers, tuberculosis and HIV/AIDS patients–bathing people who were about to die. She whispered in their ears, soothed with songs, took the time to warm the extended hands of everyone she met. With Vatican permission, she began a small order in Calcutta with only thirteen members. At the time of her death in 1997, her Missionaries of Charity included 4,000 nuns, operating 610 missions in 123 countries, including clinics, hospices, soup kitchens, counseling programs, orphanages, and schools. She only appeared in public to guide her programs. Otherwise, she avoided the limelight. She wanted people to think of Jesus, not Teresa. In daily Mass, if you didn't know where she was sitting, you wouldn't realize she was there.

Some found her devotion to the poor difficult to believe. Did she wash her hands compulsively, calling for hot water from the kitchen when her patients made do with cold? Did she ask for any other luxuries, suppress her impatience, or silence a garrulous sister so she could get on with her tasks? I can imagine in Teresa's Calcutta office a bookshelf that conceals a small chamber furnished with cot, blankets, pillow. She nods to her sisters on the way in, and they know to keep visitors away for an hour, maybe more. One shove and the bookshelf swings open. She slips inside, hurriedly dispensing with her prayers, removing her shoes, and sinking down. She draws knees to her chest, sighs like a dog, and grabs herself a selfish nap.

Others took a dim view of both her philosophy and practice. Why didn't she work toward eliminating poverty, the source of so much suffering? The *Lancet* criticized the quality of care offered in her clinics: the reuse of hypodermic needles, poor living conditions, and haphazard medical diagnosis. In the months before her death, Teresa broke her collarbone, contracted malaria, and had open-heart surgery. When she fell ill, she made the controversial decision to be treated at a well-equipped hospital in California instead of one of her own clinics. This so concerned the Archbishop of Calcutta that on her first hospitalization he ordered a priest to perform an exorcism because he thought she was under attack by the devil. Faced with an extreme model of altruism, we sanctify or turn skeptic. Following Teresa's death, the Catholic Church moved toward her canonization. Journalist Christopher Hitchens was asked to testify against her in 2002, a role he would later describe as being akin to "representing the Evil One, as it were, pro bono."

The mesolimbic pathway is a primitive area of the brain that, under MRI scans, usually lights up in response to food and sex. Neuroscientists at NIH and LABS D'Or Hospital Network decided to observe this pathway during a different kind of behavior and conducted studies with normal, healthy volunteers who placed the interests of others before their own by making charitable donations of time and money. The scientists discovered that altruistic giving ignites the very same area in the brain. They published their research in the *Proceedings of the National Academy of Sciences USA* in October 2006, noting that another brain circuit was selectively activated during the experiment: the subgenual cortex/septal region, where bonding and social attachment occur. Altruism, they suggested, is not just a superior moral faculty that suppresses basic selfish urges but is also a biological aspect hard-wired, pleasurable. It's comforting to know that Teresa might have experienced a physical bonus for her enormous kindness and sacrifice. The rest of us might also have something to look forward to if only we stopped thinking only of ourselves.

And how likely is that? Alas, the dinnertime admonishments over half-eaten succotash have disappeared and starving children in India still starve. Today, no one wants a son or daughter with low self-esteem so a false glow settles over the hair of kindergartners. Sean Penn poses in a truck bed, tossing out rice for the hungry in Haiti, and fans everywhere forgive him the vanity of his vicious temper. We commit small acts of selfishness every day: dropping scraps of toilet paper on the restroom floor, stealing Splenda packets or reams of office paper, leaving divots on the golf course to dry in the sun. Side-zooming before tollbooths, texting in movie theaters, saving a seat with our coats and purses. But spear the largest pork chop off a platter while everyone is watching? That would be uncivilized.

I can't remember if Little Miss Selfish ever came around, and the book is long out of print. In my mind she remains selfish to the end, pushing shoppers out of her way, opening other people's birthday presents. Her reward and penance are the same: eternal life in a two-dimensional, bell-shaped body, glowing golf-course green. No matter the fancy shoes and sunhat. Useless the handbag with lots of room for cash. She lives to frighten children, loathed, ridiculed.

One day a woman wakes up in the middle of her life. Her mother has died, daughter suffered a life-threatening illness, husband finally sober after a long period of abuse. Shaken, she turns in a slow, wide arc, settling uncomfortably on four decades of self-centered behavior, tempered perhaps with some tenderness toward her children, husband, very best friend. She feels appropriate shame and regret.

Good, she thinks (remembering Simone Weil), is the only real surprise.

She begins to walk daily, past her neighborhood, downtown, along the river and beyond. It's exploration, a kind of reconnaissance. Sometimes she sweeps the alleys behind houses, hoping to get a glimpse of who lives there. Corner lot grocers and bartenders are of some help. A parking lot attendant seems to know everyone. A small thing, she creates beautiful ribboned boxes filled with green tissue paper and gifts—pistachios and coffee, racetrack tickets and cologne, tobacco and licorice, a brand-new sports watch or hairclips—which she leaves on doorsteps throughout the city. On dismal mornings the old men, pissed-off mothers, painfully shy or foul-mouthed children open their doors to an unexpected lift, each box carefully tailored to their desires. They scan the sidewalks up and down, mystified.

Back home, a fire sparks in her brain, and for a while she feels illicitly high. What is this drug, and why isn't everyone doing it?

Be There No Human Here

Anthropomorphism is a way to comprehend the stars, seasons, weather, animals, any kind of nonhuman behavior. It's an ancient storytelling tool that makes life more familiar, its many dangers and losses orderly, simplified. The stars, for example–explosions of hydrogen and helium. Observing them, we have nailed down eighty-eight constellations with names like Cancer (the crab) or Orion (the hunter). Once upon a time, thunder had a human face (Jove), as did spring (Persephone). Gods on Mount Olympus were mired in human rage, jealousy, and greed. As long as we have been thinking creatures, stumbling across the earth on two legs, we've assumed human qualities could be attached to anything.

Up in the sky a pair of hawks brush the high point of my vision, imperceptibly lifting the hairs from my scalp. I lean, and lean my head back. A certain privacy surrounds them: two black accents in a field of blue, two eye motes. They follow not road signs and easements but invisible pipes, cones, funnels of wind.

To see as they see–pasture cut by road, beeches sorted from the river, weeds twitching, and then, a camouflaged mole in hyperdetail, as if under a magnifying glass. The rest of the landscape is suddenly blurred, irrelevant. To aim with just one thing in mind, even if it is, comparatively, a small mind.

And yet, how I love the gray-and-blue-tinged basin of air between us. It is like standing at the edge of a continent, a kind of reprimand: *You can't have everything. The world will always be greater than your desires.*

~~

Birds have hollow bones adapted for flight, and mammals have solid ones. I use my teeth to grind up carrots and nine-grain crackers; the chicken has a gizzard that macerates its feed. My neck seizes after ten sit-ups, and birds have extremely long and flexible cervical spines, with eleven to twenty-five cervical vertebrae instead of the average seven in mammals. See how they turn their heads and preen almost any part of their body. I tried sleeping on a train, my head leaning on the chilled, quivering window. With each gentle sway, I drifted; with each jolt, I woke. Birds have a locking mechanism that allows them to sleep with their feet perched and stable. In winter, everyone notices how pale I am, febrile, weeping from my eyes, mouth, nose, ears. A bird disguises illness as long as possible in order to avoid attack by predators. This is called "prey species defense status." For us, it could be fatal, this insistence on the appearance of health when we are failing.

Humans are the only species that can imagine a hawk's point of view, the only animals aware of our mortality. We watch a mole scamper across the field, or a grackle born with one wing, or a mallard coated with oil, and know they too are doomed. Our language is complex and varied; we invent phrases: "A byrde yn honde ys better than three yn the wode" (circa 1530) and "When you have shot one bird flying you have shot all birds flying" (Ernest Hemingway). We study, sort, place a bird in context: Kingdom: *Animalia*; Phylum: *Chordata*; Class: *Aves*;

Order: *Falconiformes*; Family: *Accipitridae*; Genus: *Buteo*; Species: *Buteo jamaicensis*. A higher degree of intelligence also allows us to build fires, cook food, clothe ourselves, as well as exchange ideas, appreciate beauty, music, art, and literature. We dream up causes for bird behavior, which doesn't mean we get it right. Pliny the Elder, for example, thought the cuckoo was just another form of the hawk, "which at a certain season of the year changes its shape; it being the fact that during this period no other hawks are to be seen, except, perhaps, for a few days only" (*Natural History*).

Out of range, a white-tailed kite swoops low over a pasture. At first we don't recognize it. How long does the bird remain an enigma? How long is our sight confused, our mind flummoxed before the imagination, and how long before a willful desire to name rushes in?

An otherwise clever man once explained to me how hummingbirds migrate to Central America: They ride the backs of geese, he said. Diminutive, fragile, light enough to be knocked out of the sky by a snowflake. Their ultrahigh metabolism requires them to eat constantly. How else would they fly such extraordinary distances? This I believed, until I couldn't. A hummingbird would freeze if it had to wait around for geese to begin their migration, right? Also, geese winter in the southern United States, so the hummers would have to dismount and transfer to another species for the rest of the journey. No one has ever observed geese whip their heads around like dogs scratching for fleas, for wouldn't they sense the hummingbirds on their backs? Finally, could a goose locate a rest stop with nutrition for both species? These are the facts as we now know them: Hummingbirds migrate long distances. *Selasphorus ru-*

fus breeds as far north as Alaska and winters in Central America, a distance of 2,700 miles. Studies have found that a male ruby-throated hummingbird, weighing about 4.5 g, of which 2 g was fat, could fly nonstop for 26 hours, consuming the fat at the rate of 0.69 calories per hour (R. C. Lasiewski, 1962).

Hummingbirds are efficient creatures; they avoid flocks, fly alone. But piggyback migration is a cozy tale and we love unlikely partnerships–think Laurel and Hardy. Thus the story persists, generation to generation.

Indeed, anthropomorphism begins in very early infancy: babies stare longer at objects that move purposefully. Later, the little tykes name their pets Sam or Molly. In school, their primary readers brim with talking cheetahs, pigs, and wolves. Not long before we see our faces on everything–a car with eyebrows, a tree with arms extending, a talking, walking robot.

Next comes the desire to control, to hold, to possess. A baby starling falls from the nest, and though it is not necessarily advisable (as it is well known, there are too many starlings–the result of one man's sentimental desire to return to England), we place "Betsy" in a towel-lined shoebox. The bird's beak is lined with yellow (like a shiny raincoat, we think). An eyedropper filled with cow's milk barely fits inside its mouth. Within hours, Betsy loses interest and dies. A bird angel arrives to take her to heaven.

We toss our very human experience over the landscape like a soggy net.

There is no caress like a parakeet's, flicking its little blue tongue over a cheek. I've learned the noises she loves: A shushing like the fall of aerated water from a faucet. Or a sustained squeaky kiss, as if I'd just eaten a sour blueberry. Most birds ignore the standard human whistle, though it's the first thing we do when we see a bird–let out a wolf whistle or a deconstructed "Happy Birthday to You." But the register is too low, too human.

I open the cage door, and after a few days of sheer terror–slamming into chandeliers, panting on the floor–the bird adjusts to my home, landing deftly on three or four strategic stations. Soon, I coax her onto my shoulder and she rides with me teetering through the house, perches on the edge of my cereal bowl, where she pecks at bananas. At my cheek, the bird is looking for salt. Between my teeth, little scraps of parsley, but I see it as affection. And what is the crime in believing my love will be returned? She sits on my shoulder and suddenly regurgitates a lump of partially digested seed. Perhaps this is her truest expression of love. She wants to feed me.

If I am close to an animal, if I love my parakeet, I will try to dissolve the differences between us. This response is sometimes called "identification," or "self-extension," and makes me prone to anthropomorphic explanations. I will imagine her continual head bobbing as pleasure at the sight of me–*yes, yes, yes*. I will name her June for the month she was born.

Here is an extended example of how we've captured another particular species for our cultural shorthand:

I've got to go, can you manage by yourself? Yes, I have my blackbird right here in my pocket. A blackbird is a nickname for a small black handgun.

Or, a blackbird is a girl who puts on a happy face, but collapses in private: *Have you seen her room? Ever since her sister died, Sarah's been hiding out there; she's a total blackbird.*

FBI, ATF, CIA, or DEA agents are called blackbirds. They'll tap your phone. This is known as "blackbird on the wire." *Is this a good time to talk? Wait, no, I think I hear something . . .*

A blackbird is a sleek, black, highly advanced U.S. spy plane that currently holds the record for the highest ceiling and fastest plane ever to fly. You won't see it from your porch, or even in the middle of a field. Ever.

Where's Steph? I saw her a minute ago. She must have blackbirded out of here. To blackbird is to leave a party surreptitiously without saying good-bye. Something to think about when you're tired, when you've had enough of the chatter.

We're a long way from *Agelaius phoeniceus*, the raucous species common to farm and field, predisposed to hassling hawks. We spot a red-winged blackbird swaying on a telephone wire and drag it down, fold it into our slang, our secret codes. The blackbird becomes a versatile tool, employed by criminals, aviators, teenagers, and cops.

Maybe there's more to our urge to humanize feathered creatures—anthropomorphism likely a subconscious reflection of what we share with them, a primitive kinship. Birds can be traced back to a series of reptilian groups called the *Synapsida*, which evolved over an approximately 100 million year period from the Pennsylvanian to the end of the Triassic, when true mammals appeared. The National Human Genome Research

Institute (NHGRI) has shown that chickens and humans have in common more than half of their genes, some two thousand genes involved in the cell's basic structure and function. The avian skeleton too resembles in some ways the human skeleton: humerus + radius + ulna. Femur + tibia + fibula. Cranium + maxilla + mandible. Tailbone. The majority of bones are the same; others are fused or shaped differently.

Birdsong has its parallel in humans. Genes tell both species to learn the language of their own kind, and no other. And neither bird nor baby immediately master communication: fledgling white-crowned sparrows and humans listen before they begin to speak. The sparrow will first sing a short subsong derived from a tutor's full song. The young bird keeps practicing this little bit of nonsense just as infants practice their words. When my daughter Bonnie was little, she fixed on the sound of *cheese* and repeated other words in the same sound family: please, these, keys, peas, leaves. Later–full song, full sentences. "Cheese please! Throw your keys in the leaves!"

Raised in Kentucky, she acquired a slight drawl. *Bye* becomes "Ba." *Hair* becomes "hay-er." Sparrows too have a dialect, depending on where they live. Don Kroodsma, reigning authority on the biology of bird vocal behavior, tours the country by bicycle, listening to Steller's jays in California, house wrens in Tennessee, warblers in Georgia, towhees in New England. He recorded and analyzed hundreds of songs and concluded that where a bird learned a song is just as important as a bird's genealogy. Later, he recorded human accents as well and is confident we can tell a lot about where either species was born by its burr, twang, brogue, or nasality.

At his large kitchen window, a retired man settles down in a cloud of morning lint and rumpled skin. He gathers a legal pad, his five-hundred-dollar Montblanc fountain pen, a stained cup of Postum. He combs the backyard for a way into his masterpiece, the poem that finally will make *Yankee Magazine*, maybe even the *New Yorker*. Outside, a line of suet feeders hang from a porch beam, rocked by the larger birds, pecked and beloved by all species. He begins, "The titmouse, all nerves and ambition. . . ."

Birds strike the window at least once a week, falling to the deck in limp feather-clusters. He always checks: dazed or dead, one or the other. To ease his conscience he wraps the dead ones in plastic sandwich bags, stores them in the freezer, and later drops them off at the university's biology department. Unwittingly, he has created the perfect conditions for mold and accelerated rot. He cannot know that an expert folds the head under a wing and inserts the bird into a nylon stocking, which makes a firm but airy case for freezing. He doesn't know his specimens go directly in the trash.

A panel of sunshine breaks into the garden and for the first time he notices the buff patch under the titmouse's wing "like blush on a woman's cheek." His wife again. Every morning he searches his cabinet for shaving cream and there's her makeup in a heap. But wait, this sounds new: "its crest moves like a retractable surgical knife." No, "its crest retracts like a miniature box cutter."

He cannot imagine the flock of birdfeeder poems that alight every day on magazine editors' desks.

Is it possible to watch a red-breasted merganser jut its head back and forth without thinking of Daffy Duck? Can we observe a foraging pileated without the Woody Woodpecker "car-tune" idling somewhere deep in our brain?

A table is covered with oilcloth, long benches on either side. In neat piles: scalpels, looped flesher tools, curved hemostats, acid brushes, borax/sawdust mixture, needles, thread, cotton balls, and tubs of pink formaldehyde paste. Six students are wearing aprons and sterile gloves, and each prepares herself with a precise mental distance: a hospital curtain in one mind, an imaginary suit of mail in another. One boy summons the nonchalance of nitrous from a dentist's chair, where he managed to be both alert and relaxed.

As if they sat in a street-side café, their leader offers a tray with an array of species to choose from, all of them common: purple grackle, three house sparrows, blue jay, cowbird, titmouse, and starling. No one chooses the starling, with its stunted tail and apocalyptic foreboding.

The bird is positioned belly up, and each student blows with little puffs till feathers part and the breastbone is revealed. Along this, the first incision—from tail to beak—feather membrane separated from the body sack and scraped clean till the bird is turned inside-out. It's slow work, careful, as the membrane is easily torn and no one wants to cover a sloppy job with a pile of stitches. Excavating the skull comes next and here the students heap on the sawdust; the smell is something else and plucking brain tissue with a hemostat or tweezers requires a little more than an imaginary curtain. Two girls have successfully swallowed their disgust but now have a desperate need to go to the bathroom.

It's a good point for a break anyway–sip Cokes in silence–then back to the table. Turn the bird on its stomach and continue gently pulling, scraping tendons, legs, wings, the skin spread out, and finally, painted pink. The rest is home economics. Balls of cotton are stretched and molded around a stick to fill the cavity. Two tiny knots for the eyes. Overhand stitches with heavy black thread, repairs to any torn membrane. One girl, shaping the belly, thinks of the Little Prince's drawing of a snake after it swallowed an animal whole. Bird and snake resemble a kind of rounded desert plateau, or one of those American Indian burial mounds. Still, she is a long, long way from Glow Worm and Ollie the elephant, beloved stuffed animals of her youth.

Kingdom: *Animalia*; Phylum: *Chordata*; Subphylum: *Vertebrata*; Class: *Mammalia*; Order: *Primates*; Family: *Hominidae*; Genus: *Homo*; Species: *Homo sapiens*. Latin *homo*, meaning "man"; or *hem*–"the earthly one" (as in *humus*). Latin *sapiens*, meaning "wise" or "knowing."

The International Union for the Conservation of Nature lists *Homo sapiens* as a species of least concern for extinction.

Lake Mattamuskeet Wildlife Refuge in North Carolina: A group of amateur birdwatchers arrive from Washington, D.C.

–chubby, middle-aged, suburbanite men and women who don't mind getting up at the crack of dawn. Necks hung with binoculars, eyes and faces lifted to the sky, they are escorted around the lake every day for a week. Their guide is an awkward, chapped-lipped young man who does this only because it earns a living and allows him to be outdoors with the birds. Obviously, he keeps a life list, glued to the back cover of his Peterson's. He passes it around, evidence of his obsession, a collection, he explains, that doesn't require ownership. It's migration season and he encourages the group to expand their own lists with open ears and acute attention to the smallest quiver under a leaf. The warblers alone, in alphabetical order: American redstart, black-and-white warbler, blackpoll warbler, black-throated green warbler, Canada warbler, common yellowthroat, hooded warbler, Nashville warbler, northern parula, northern waterthrush, orange-crowned warbler, ovenbird, palm warbler, pine warbler, prairie warbler, prothonotary warbler, yellow-breasted chat, yellow-rumped warbler, yellow-throated warbler. This kind of diversity can't be found everywhere. Still, about half of the group sees this tour around the lake as a social occasion, lagging back, chattering.

Was he irritated when a cough startled a black-throated blue lighting briefly on its way down the Atlantic Flyway to South America? When a twig snapped under a dull boot? When one of the women tossed her string-cheese wrapper into the grass? Humans are heavy, loud, dense, and preoccupied. Their bodies obvious, oblivious, obstructing. He loves the mystery of a 55,000-acre swamp next to the sea that reveals only a little of itself at a time. He prefers solitude, the dank canvas of a bird blind muting his own rude shape, its gross movements and sounds. He tries to breathe noiselessly.

Be there no human here
be there here the flat marsh
before man, be there here

those bony wings.
("Window Views," Laura Jensen)

Every night I dream of flying. My arms pump laboriously; I rise six or seven feet above the pursuant tiger, bear, serpent. Something is always chasing me. There's no safe place on the compound, though I lurch from barn to garage to precarious rooster-cupola. Sometimes I make it as far as the upper canopy of sycamores, catching my breath till the predator appears, thumping on the ground below. The sky is an unreal indigo. My clothes weigh me down, as if I were swimming through Karo syrup. Of the many styles of dream flying, I always revert to the breaststroke, using my hands for guidance at the beginning of each backward pull. Fatigue is a serious limitation.

Oh, to be like my husband, waking each morning dazzled, his dream flight a green-glass liberation. He describes a pin, or Superman-style: horizontal, arms straight before him, hips tilting slightly to steer. The worst he can remember is flying too high, beyond the sound of human voice, siren, even explosion. Ice crystals formed on his fingertips and eyelashes. His lips cracked and burned. Finally, he executed a midair reverse flip, which got him going in the right direction.

Flying dreams are related to the vestibular system, which regulates body equilibrium. I read this somewhere. Also, that sleep clinics have actually induced these dreams by manipulating the sleeper's sense of balance: applying a blood-pressure cuff, rocking in a hammock, raising and lowering the bed.

But why is it so hard to get off the ground? Maybe I'm just exhausted, still processing some unsettling news from my sister. Or perhaps my marrow-stuffed bones are just too heavy, even in my imagination. Real bird bones are filled with air. Birds have no teeth, another adaptation that makes them lighter.

I often dream my own teeth are crumbling and falling to my hands. But it doesn't make flying any easier for me.

A mist net is black, made of nylon, and resembles an extremely fine volleyball net. Ornithologists stretch them across thickets, deep in forests, and along shorelines in darkness or nearly moonless nights to capture birds in flight. They are almost invisible. Hitting a mist net, most birds tumble into a pocket of mesh, which quickly folds around them. They will suffer from wind, rain, and possibly predation if left for long periods of time, so it's vital that nets are checked often. Each bird tangled in mesh presents a unique challenge in extraction. We run the risk of strangling them—though there is no soft spot in the bird's trachea that can collapse (as in mammals), overconstriction of the entire body during restraint can cause oxygen deprivation. If we are worried the bird will escape, or frustrated at the snarl of fine threads around a wing, we might apply unnecessary force. If the bird struggles too much, the tangles inevitably worsen. Practice, extra care, patience, and common sense are needed to free a bird. In worst-case scenarios, we can always grab a pocketknife or pair of scissors.

Avoiding the risks of mist nets altogether, pull traps, drop traps, and walk-in traps are also available to capture ground-feeding species.

Now a mourning dove waddles into a walk-in, lured by a heap of sunflower seeds and millet, and catches the wire mechanism. The trap snaps shut, and I approach cautiously so as not to further fluster the bird. It will hurl itself against the wire mesh relentlessly in the effort to escape, tearing tissue, feathers. I slide up the door, spread the left hand over the opening, then reach into the cage to embrace the dove with the right, grasping the body without squeezing, careful to envelop each wing, its head nestled gently between index and middle fingers. I pass the dove through the rubber flaps of a keeping cage and carry the cage inside, where an assistant removes and holds the bird firmly. I gently extend the leg, press a number-stamped metal ring around with a tool that prevents overlap; record in a loose-leaf binder that number, date, species, gender, any unusual features; walk the bird outside myself, open my hand and . . .

To our surprise, the dove doesn't take flight immediately. It pauses, as though unbelieving. Shock at the sudden breeze when, before, death had a scent, sensation–salty, warm, and unyielding. Seconds pass.

No, I take back the "unbelieving," "shock at the sudden breeze," the impression that "death had a scent, sensation." I think instead: *All the lives I could live, all the species I will never know, never will become–they are everywhere. That is what the world is.*

The bird flies, with an audible whistling sound.

P E R *f* E C T
Barn

Having all the required or desirable elements, qualities,
or characteristics; as good as it is possible to be.

Who named it perfect? Who made the declaration? Was it a
swallow, nest mud-plastered to a piece of solid timber? Dried
herbs sprouting a cottony mold? Rain that slides in sheets down
the red tin roof? Wasps that appreciate ventilation but would
never tell you so? Folding chairs in need of a stiff brush and
paint? The straw, the long-dead horse, and its hocked saddle?
The *what* that will take the place of rakes, dangerously rusting
in a webby corner?

Soon I'll move my chair, or run inside for oranges, or fail to
sleep very well, and then humidity will lay a green slime across
the siding. The barn will not resist. In this the barn is no better
than fence, or catalpa, or fields of medium-brown wheat.

But for now, the barn has perfect siding the color of coffee
grounds flecked with salt and a long gray wind-stroking. The
door doesn't fit and I love it so, love the shoulder lift I must perform in freeing it from its lock. I'm a little frightened of teta-

nus but the bottom gap that brushes grass and hedgebrook sets forth a minty smell. The tractor on blocks, the barn's ambling house-shape with hexagonal door frames. Above, parabolas of bird-hunger chasing mosquitoes. There's an easy reason for the barn's abandonment. I love holding that reason back.

Woman Drawn Twice

Laura, elder daughter of two, driver of a Toyota as old as she is, occupant of the attic room, is going off to college. My friends are all sympathetic. I must be a bad parent because this imminent separation doesn't strike me as tragic.

What's made it easier is Laura herself. She holds the world at arm's length. Even as a baby, Laura would allow only her father and me to touch her. Uncles and aunts, forget it. Her very first sentence was, as I tried to pry loose the flap from her diaper, "Don't do that!"

Once we went camping and she brought her friend Rita along. For three days they were inseparable, sunbathing together on the rocks, hiking into town for sliders and French fries. Then suddenly Laura had enough social bonding. She began to sleep in, to disappear on mysterious after-dinner strolls. I took my tea to the edge of the creek one morning, and there was poor Rita, splashing about in a canoe, forlorn and abandoned.

Laura keeps a journal, leaves it on the coffee table or on the bathroom floor. Perhaps to lure us inside, perhaps not. But we don't look. She also has a web page and there with a click of a button we are welcomed in, browsers like anyone else. It doesn't feel like trespassing, but the voice we hear is not meant for her parents:

> Hello beautiful this is Laura the 16 year old illegal permit driving, Manual High School attending, singing, dancing, romancing Ramsi's employee. I read, write, and wish everyday that precalculus didn't exist. I'm out every weekend, sorry to you silly fools that get online 24/7 no I don't want to be your friend. Why do people love those bland, uninteresting talentless "artists" they see on television? That was cynical . . . and no im not a lesbian. Im going to NYU to be an English professor of creative writing with three novels, a wealthy, but interesting husband im in love with and a kid or two in my spare time. You have a problem with it you can call my super expensive top of the line lawyer, wherever she is.

Laura the timid one, the make-a-fort-in-the-closet girl, the girl who never wore shorts much less a bathing suit?

As a teenager, I was pure ham: spoke, sang, even whispered at high volume. No matter how subtle or insignificant the emotion, I embellished it, stealing from performances I'd seen on TV, exaggerating until my audience was drawn in. At sixteen, I told my mother everything and opened my heart to anyone else who would listen too. Because in my mind, a kept secret was a festering thought, dangerous to my health.

My mother was a guardian of secrets, gentle soldier at the kitchen sink, doe with ears twitching. Always a listener, ever available, her own dark thoughts settled deep, pushed there by the flutter-kick of family. When it came time for my college lift-off, things went smoothly. A long drive west on the pitted Pennsylvania turnpike, then Ohio, steaming in late August heat. I remember this: Luggage in hand, we approached Cory Hall, my dorm for a semester. What an eyesore–tattered vinyl sofas in the lobby, graffiti on the cinderblock walls, gray-green drapes half up, half down. Something evil and stinky dripped from a balcony above. We had to dodge it to get in. "Oh, Sarah," my mother said, her voice drooping. But this midwestern hippie school was my choice and it had to be a good one, so I chirped, "It's OK!" And I followed two longhaired boys up the stairs. When I glanced back, she was gone.

I see my mother's orange VW bus pull into the driveway and she enters the house again. There on the counter, the smoked turkey I love between two slices of Wonder Bread. There my jeans with their U.S. flag patches that caused such an argument. Now the hairclips, Prell shampoo, and mildewed camping equipment. Wandering from room to room, she gathers up the debris. She soaks up the silence and wonders why the storm that was her daughter's adolescence felt so difficult to navigate.

But I am just imagining things. Perhaps she simply turns to the next child, Nancy, with less than two years to go.

Laura has lost her sculpture, which at first glance resembles a stone thumb. Upon closer inspection, it's actually quite moving–a tiny figure stooped in prayer or under the weight of a great burden. She kept it in a shoebox on the stairs, but now only the sandpaper and tools are in evidence. She's frantic and of course it's all my fault, "Your incessant cleaning, Mom. Tomorrow the sculpture is due in 3D art!"

Turns out the dog carried it outside and is happily gnawing on the little penitent. We approach him and he rumbles low in his throat.

Laura in the backseat, complaining about Cézanne. "I think his paintings are ugly. He's way overrated. His portrait of the Alps looks like a big lump of ham." My husband suggests she look at his other work before she condemns him completely. "Yeah, yeah," she drones. "I'm sick of the Impressionists. Public schools love them. Humanities and Impressionism. French and Impressionism. Art and Impressionism. Blah Impressionism Blah."

> *Poor little melon, tossed in with the black turnips.*
> —CHINESE PROVERB

Years earlier, while Laura "napped" in her big-girl bed, we'd hear a complex drama in several voices, high and low. "Jesus, I'm making a lot of noise," she remarked. Later, when she began to read, the theater went deeper inside. Folded up like a frog under her kindergarten desk, she breezed through all of Roald Dahl. Her teacher reported this with a wry smile, then added generously, "OK with me, as long as she's reading." By early adolescence it was *Sanctuary*, *Laughter in the Dark*, and *Light in August*. At twelve, she showed us her first short story, "Climbing Out," written for an English class, about a girl who leaves a bad relationship with her boyfriend. We were surprised by its sophistication—the wry, clear voice from one so young:

Eric stood up and climbed into the back of his '97 Ford pickup truck, his jeans clinging to the Tommy Hilfiger emblem on his boxer shorts. I had been dating Eric for over eight months and not once during that time had he ever used a belt. His idea of good conversation was a discussion on the gayness of our history teacher, Mr. Higgens.

"Hey Liz, what about his new toupee, is the horsehair real or faux do you suppose?" he called from the truck.

His pointed smile reminded me of the Trix rabbit. "Go stand in the snow," I replied.

She'd never even had a boyfriend, as far as I knew.

My mother had a literary life. I know because I discovered her thesis, red-leather bound, carbon-copied on onionskin—Peggy Aring's analysis of Melville's *Billy Budd*. I know because of the pencil marks in her Modern Library edition of Frost and Dickinson, her poems around their poems. She read widely—Rexroth's translations, Snyder, Williams, of course. She leaned toward the aesthetics of haiku master Takahama Kiyoshi, who believed that when a poet's sentiments are overly visible, the audience grows uncomfortable. Better to write simply and only what is *there* in a scene, to make a connection by calling on a reader's imagination. Her pencil crossed and recrossed phrases that struck her as sentimental or melodramatic.

One day a tall, gangly, middle-aged poet named Donald Petersen showed up at our front door. In his book from Wesleyan University Press, which he was carrying, he called her his muse.

"And did you know she wrote too?" he said to me. My mother flushed and wished him away. The poor man never made it inside the house, though he had traveled for several hours.

She wouldn't want me to tell you. But for the life of me, I can't keep a secret.

My husband, a collector, purchases a "safety pen" circa 1904, its case sterling, about three-quarters of an inch in diameter. It looks like a fancy cigar tube, but twist a knob at the base and the fourteen-carat gold nib emerges from the chamber. Twist again, and it spirals back, undetectable.

An hour of solitude in my house occupied by teenagers. It's three in the afternoon. I'm relishing *Carmen* on my radio, an arrangement for flute and piano. It speeds up my thinking, makes me want to dance. Laura is just now waking up.

She appears puffy-eyed at my study door in her Cabbage Patch pajamas. "Mom. *Mom*. MOM. Would you turn that music off? It sounds like 'Pop Goes the Weasel.' Why would you wanna hear that first thing in the a.m.?"

By dinner Laura has noticed it's Mother's Day and has finally pulled something together. She swipes one of my greeting cards and attaches a tulip, snipped from a bouquet I purchased that morning to cheer myself up. Later, feeling a little sheepish, she leaves a pot of petunias on the front hallway floor. "Is this for me?" I have to ask.

———

I scour the literature. Romain Rolland: "The child absorbs such a lot of lies and foolish nonsense, mixed in with essential truths, that the first duty of the adolescent who wants to be healthy is to disgorge it all." What Rolland and others neglect to say is how well adolescence readies the *parent* for separation. As if every transition from one stage of life to another demands a trail of stones and potholes, crests and gorges to be truly effectual. Here's one verse to that song: "Why are you always harping on me? Do you have to eat right next to me? Why don't you make Bonnie walk the dog? Why do you have to chew so loud?"

In Chinese characters *woman* drawn twice signifies "quarrel."

Laura is working at Baskin-Robbins four days a week, despite her intention to "be as irresponsible as I can this summer." Spare time is spent sleeping, on the computer IMing her friends, shopping at thrift stores. Obligation to family or chores gets short shrift. So too, eating. The bowl of muddy milk left on the living room floor—Cocoa Krispies and skim—is the only evidence she's had any sustenance at all.

The pendulum begins to swing. *Back*. My mother was ashamed of her body. *Forth*. I kept a list of lovers in a little black notebook. *Back*. My mother picked at her food, content with the turkey back, the wing. *Forth*. I claimed the white meat, ate ravenously. Now, I stand guard over Laura to make sure she finishes her dinner. I thump pointlessly on the bathroom door, the only place she can lock herself in.

"Why are you such a Hitler?" she asks.

Laura and Rita want to drive to Morehead to camp, this time without us. Oh my. The eastern Kentucky woods in an unreliable, eighteen-year-old Toyota Tercel. The morning news influences our decision: A stripper in New Jersey pulled off the road when her car broke down. As she checked under the hood, she was blindsided by a passing vehicle. The driver kept going. So did the next three, even after they felt the jolt of her body under their wheels.

And the young man accepted at Yale who fell asleep at the wheel and careened over a cliff in Colorado. And teenagers and country roads without yellow lines. And the dark, and the dark beer they'll surely be drinking. And Laura last year on the spearmint lake at Disney World in her own little powerboat careening about like a demented waterbug. Rocks, pilings, piers. A ferry's boiling wake. Other unpredictable boats. And Laura traversing the waterfall, Laura with her nonchalant springy step, her inexplicable mixture of shyness and daring. Her parents holding their breath.

So: No. No, sorry, no. While your father and I can still say it. No.

My mother said no too, and I trotted downstairs to my bedroom with its strung-up Christmas ornament like a modern-day gazing ball. Then I cranked the little wheel on my window and slipped out to Rob and his van, his pot, our brand-new sex under maniacal cicadas in the dense Washington night.

When Laura comes home one night with a red mark like a

Luden's lozenge at the base of her neck, I feel justified. She was supposed to be sleeping at Danielle's house. Just who gave her the hickey? Danielle? Not that I have a leg to stand on, which is why my outrage is tinged with hilarity. The Chinese said it first: children are creditors collecting for the sins of our past lives.

Again, I have the dream, not uncommon among women. Back at college for the summer term. The Ohio heat is suffocating, grass brown and rigid as toothpicks. Students less than half my age move about without even a glance in my direction. I'm not interesting; I'm too old to be here. But I've forgotten to turn in my paper for some literature class, or take that last PE credit (here the details vary), so my degree is at risk. Where's my family, everything I've accomplished? I'm nothing and the countryside too has lost its landmarks, uniform beige surrounding the college like Beirut.

My husband and I agree that Laura needs more than her public-school-twenty-four-year-old-baseball-coach-disaster-of-an-English-teacher can provide. We sign her up for the Reynolds Young Writers Workshop at Denison University, where she will study with Erin McGraw, a real fiction writer. She receives a large scholarship and before we know it, we're in the airport gently pressing a reluctant sixteen-year-old toward the boarding gate. She won't let us kiss her good-bye, annoyed that we've forced her into this. But a quick glance before she disappears into the plane reveals all–she's terrified. I let my husband drive home, too upset, convinced we should never have forced her into this. "Never have ideas about children," said D. H. Lawrence. "Never have ideas *for* them."

Three days pass and her first email finally arrives from Denison. Subject heading: "Blue Haired Freaks Can Suck My Bumper."

> Family! How are things la? Last evening Erin McGraw gave a reading from her unpublished new novel. We are the first ever to hear the opening chapter. She is an amazing writer and even with the typically short attention span that dominated this particular audience, every one of us listened with awe. My story is going to be workshopped on Sunday. I'm really struggling with this one. I need to concentrate on the plot now, as opposed to character but I made the mistake of writing it in the first person instead of third. . . . OH, and at 2:00 a.m. we TPed the TA lounge and called random room numbers unpleasantly waking anyone who'd gone to bed.

She was knee deep in the joy of an unmanufactured epiphany. On the phone she gushed: "I've learned more in one day than I did in four years at Manual. Dad, do you know David Foster Wallace or Lorrie Moore or Marilynne Robinson? They are my heroes." Denison was just the sort of experience she needed to anchor the indefinite future. Now she had a road sign to set her sights on.

On July 30, 1980, during one of the hottest summers in D.C.

history, my mother died of cervical cancer. Most cases are curable; this one moved to her lymph nodes and beyond shortly after diagnosis. She was just fifty-one. Her legs and arms puffed with fluid; her belly bulged under the sheet as if she were six months pregnant. For over a month, my sisters and I had shared the task of keeping her comfortable. We said our goodbyes in caretaking–washing her hair, poaching the egg she would never eat, reading E. B. White's letters out loud, transcribing her farewell notes, which amounted to just a few words each in virtually all–"Please know how much I care about you. So very sorry to bring this into your life." She declined medical treatment, hastened the end by refusing to sip ice water from the tumbler we set on her bedside table. After five days of this, her irises glittered an unnatural ice blue. Her intention was to make things easier for us, but it meant there was little opportunity for the many questions we had. And no time of course for future weddings, careers, accomplishments she could share. After she was gone, I kissed her cooling forehead. It seemed as conclusive a farewell as there could be.

Little did I know that in dreams and daylight visions, she would return again, a diminished version of herself. She dressed in a blue-and-white-striped garden apron, jeans, and clogs. A mother with a prolonged cold, a chronic disease, but reasonably content in her new life. She lived in Portugal, in Southern France, or lately, in Newfoundland. Once I could feel her hanging onto the roof of our Toyota as we sped up the coast to Connecticut.

And now she appears in Laura's long legs, splayed feet, and angled posture. My mother's chiseled Lutheran nose catches me by surprise when Laura cuts her bangs, or ties back her hair.

She hates to hear this stuff, doesn't want to be associated with a dead person she never knew.

Besides, there's a difference. Next summer Laura will circle back, but not as a ghost, not a diminished, but an enlarged being. This reassures and unsettles me, for isn't it the natural order? And, isn't it my place she's taking?

In the new and improved dorm room at Laura's college, complete with microwave oven, tiny refrigerator, and private bathroom (tuition has increased by 700 percent since I went to school), I'll be steeled for the big moment. I don't expect much—a ritual peck on the cheek, which she will instantly wipe off.

I'll drive the van home, park under the silver maple, if I'm lucky and there's a spot. The house will be much the same as before. There, the crumbs from her onion bagel and video games spread out on the floor. She never did learn to put them away. There, the OxiClean, Q-tips, spray of face powder across the sink. The ubiquitous collapsed pajamas. I'm not imagining things—she's gone, and the time for grieving is underway.

Or, perhaps I'll turn to her sister Bonnie, ready to inherit Laura's room, her car, her status as the grown-up one. Bonnie, with less than two years to go.

$$\left\{ \quad \text{P E R } f \text{ E C T} \quad \right\}$$
$$\textit{Heaven}$$

When my mother died, I began to smoke Kents, as she had during difficult times. It didn't last long. I was never a determined smoker.

I tried to pray with absolute attention. I enjoyed the Our Father for its symmetry: "on earth / as it is in heaven," and "forgive us our trespasses / as we forgive those who trespass against us." But my mind rambled. By "now and forever," I was making a list for the hardware store, wondering which fertilizer would save the Japanese maple by our front porch. A more practical kind of consolation.

If only I knew her intimate habits and feelings. Then the space she left behind would not seem so stark.

I pictured her figure open to the elements, birds plucking bits of cotton, skin, hair, carrying them off to line their nests. Rain drawing her blood into the soil; tissue, tendon, and muscle battered with air. Finally bone, returned to its chemical components and scattered like microscopic hail.

Perhaps a body is perfect not when it is complete but when there is no longer anything to take away.

I can't recall my mother singing. Not even a shout or robust coughing. Was she preoccupied by minute workings of blood through her temples, an ear filament flaring out, or cells turning mean, flipped over to their dark side like microscopic playing cards?

When I think of my mother's inner life, I see a Kleenex, its powdery edges twisted into sculpture. She gripped it while the party wound down.

After she died, I removed a crumpled one from her purse. Dry, but sudden too, as a splash in my hand.

Maybe heaven is textured like a river after it falls over rocks. Maybe it is nothing. Perhaps we are suppressed or superreal. Unaccompanied, or linked by our hair to everyone who has died.

My mother was given twelve baby-shaped beans to hold tightly as she went over, the grandchildren she would not meet in this life.

Burn her sweaters, party shoes, and skirts so she can wear them if she wants.

Neriage, or What Is the
Secret of a Long Marriage?

Once upon a time, a lump of clay was lifted from the earth by human hands. The clay was rolled into a sphere, a wormy coil, then squashed flat again with fingers and toes.

Marianne Ellison was born in 1892, in Hamburg, New York. She weighed just six pounds and immediately began to peer around. All was light and shadow, but fascinating.

Henry Piper was born two years later, a few doors down from Marianne. He had a crown of thick black hair and an operatic voice that carried down the corridor and into the street.

Because clay is impure, it must be kneaded, or "wedged," with a steady pushing and rocking motion. Sometimes a bubble appears in the conchlike folds, spreads, weakens, finally bursts. Seeds, pebbles, roots, pinecone chips like curses or objections, all dispersed. The clay is soon homogenized, filled with a mysterious energy, smooth and springy as the predawn surface of a pond.

Marianne was a precocious child and an even more impressive adult. Her qualities? A tendency to react quickly, flushing deep scarlet all the way up to her ears. An inability to sit still, rising from her seat four times at least during a meal to grab silverware, wine, or water. A penchant for collecting miniatures, for organizing, for saving her favorite part of a meal for last. A love of short novels that satisfied but allowed her to get on with her day. Moving, doing, perseverance, loyalty.

Henry's graces? Charm, social ease, a sense of humor that mixed low with the elevated. An addiction to music, tobacco, meat, bread, sugar. Extreme focus, whether the task be budget percentages, bicycle routes, or the repair of a screen door. Builder of bookcases. Forgetter of birthdays, errands, and the names of relatives beyond his primary family. Watching, being, intelligence, big hands.

Imagine a landscape of one continuous hue. Imagine clay fired year after year to a monotonous brown. It wasn't long before someone thought to add iron, cobalt, manganese, creating difference—pattern and color. *Neriage*, a Japanese term meaning "to mix," involves blending layers of multicolored clay to form teapots, vases, bowls, any vessel a person might wish.

Black is Saturn, diamonds, lead, error, falsehood, in blazonry— prudence and constancy. Red is Mars, fortitude, divine love, the metal of war, rubies, martyrdom, charity. Neriage is a wedding of opposites, hot and cold, flexible and resolute.

Marianne first met her neighbor Henry by a pond brimming with duckweed and tree frogs. She was seventeen, he fifteen, and each was seeking reprieve from the inner weather of their respective homesteads. Born of preacher and postman, respectively, Marianne and Henry were known villagewide as the independent sort, remarkable for their curiosity and acumen.

They married in a garden, surrounded by Portlandia, Star of the Nile, Will-o'-the-Wisp, though the roses were burlap-bundled against the cold. Marianne wore a black skirt with matching jacket. Henry's suit was also plain, his one reckless move a crimson handkerchief. Their Lutheran minister had reservations about the young couple. Could they endure what lay ahead? It was storming in the South, though the rain held off for their simple ceremony.

Side by side:

her reticence	his humor
her acceptance	his suspicion
her optimism	his irony

Neriage is all about parceling out the goods fairly, then putting them back together. In the beginning were stripes, then checkerboard, pinwheels, zigzag, and so forth. Finally, the highly complex *bokuryu*, or "flowing ink" style. But most patterns begin with two colors of opposing hue, hunks of red and black clay, sliced with a cutting wire into slabs. Positioned on lengths of clean canvas. Intact, separate.

It was as if each room were divided into two.

Her space was small, formal, sharp cornered. A bookcase behind the door, diaries and novels piled on every available surface, but artfully, like fancy cakes. Two ancient desks arranged into a practical L: one in dark-stained oak, the other English pine with a worn spot where a farmer once rested his foot. On the wall, she hung printer's boxes to display her miniscule teapots, scissors, spoons, and thimbles. *Everything in its place. This is not The Box!* (What exactly did that mean, printed in bold?) She longed for a dictionary stand.

His territory was more complicated. Drawings, drafts, and pithy tributes gathered dust in boxes—his desk no longer visible for the piles of books and crumpled paper. Even his leather bag bubbled and gushed with wire-rimmed reading glasses, file folders, mail he simply couldn't bear to throw away. He bought clocks and toy cars on special order, setting some of them aside for resale. Though not obvious to the observer, he had a system. Once he found a tax-refund check for $116 he'd used for a bookmark, now several years beyond its expiration date.

Initially, the clay resists fusion. Some say pigments are to blame, each a unique chemistry that encourages autonomy, insularity. Others claim the slabs have begun, quite naturally, to mature—an hour of clay time is two years in human time. As it interacts with air, dust, water, each piece develops a skin, a definite self-sufficiency.

Saturday morning, before the chores were done:

> –What a mess. How can you live like this. Why don't you throw this stuff away.
> –It's my mess. Please get out of my mess.
> –But your mess is all over the place. Can't you clean it up?
> –It's my mess. Leave my mess alone.

Sometimes he sketched, spread out on her couch, coffee mug in a liquid mocha ring on her bookshelf, shoes splayed, socks bunched up, then she didn't know what to do with herself and skittered back and forth like a child unseated in a game of musical chairs. He was startled to find his cars arranged in a parade across the windowsill, polished to a military shine. She had ruined them! One night, he was forced outside under the stars to dig through the trash for an early draft of a speech that now seemed better than the revision. In a burst of cleaning, she'd tossed it out.

Ethologist Jean-Jacques Petter recognized the human need for rivalry, naming it *noyau*, or "society of inward antagonism," which like an alloy, gains strength from the interior clash and meld of dissimilar components. Paul Fussell calls it the "versus habit." The Japanese have in-yō.

Masters of neriage understand that art and love both begin with violence. They put aside their squeamishness and break the clay's resistance–desecrating, or scoring, each slab. A fork does the quickest work, the sharper the better. Scraped vertically, horizontally, no corner left untouched. Then sweep a damp brush coated with slip over the cut surface, softening, coaxing.

For Marianne, it was the loss of her mother, who died of tuberculosis. A stubborn woman, she was fearful of hospitals and allowed the disease to advance unimpeded. Marianne loved her immeasurably, had so much left to ask, and yet stood by helplessly as her mother lay parched and rasping on the bed. For Henry the pivotal event was his sister's suicide by drowning, though tragically, she was an excellent swimmer. After a week of searching, she was found in neighboring Lake Muscatine, fully clothed, bricks and big stones in her coat pockets. In both cases, the funerals were private functions, though friends slipped boxes of food, notes, and flowers onto their porch. One left a basket containing a bulldog pup, whom they embraced, naming him Arthur.

Over the years adversity continued on and off, tearing, tempering. Henry and Marianne nearly lost their first child to peritonitis; their second fell in love with a destructive boy, who eventually committed a murder. Marianne developed early arthritis. At the tender age of forty, she found herself unable to write by hand, though she could type, pecking with one or two fingers. Henry was stalked by an unstable student, a war veteran, who finally had to be institutionalized.

There was good fortune too: an invitation to study in Rome, a financial windfall from a state granting program, newborn nieces, nephews. Their youngest was the first in her class to attend an out-of-state university with a full scholarship. She made the transition from small town to busy metropolis brilliantly, sending postcards full of exclamation points. The eldest set up a law practice in town, the only lawyer who would, when necessary, accept paintings, a dental exam, or a half-hog in lieu of payment. Marianne and Henry enjoyed his bounty too, filling their freezer with frozen raspberries and tubs full of chicken rice soup.

her outbursts	his restraint
her anxiety	his faith
her flexibility	his willfulness

The masters instruct: Nestle red on black, black on red. Listen for the suck of connection, they explain. Slice a new set of slabs, score, brush with slip, repeat, repeat, repeat, until you have a tower of red and black. Compress with the force of a hard rain, a good freeze. Flip the stack onto its side, pile up your shims, and once more, draw your wire through the clay. This is the aha moment when the singular pattern reveals itself. Note how well the stripes have knit together, elongating, swaying like geological striations or Venetian marbled paper.

After time and sufficient pressure, any boundary will fail to hold up. Unpatrolled, they leak, tributaries of river silt irrigating the fields, tendrils of campfire creeping across the dirt. Human characteristics too–of habit, perception, even physical appearance–leap their borders, muddy the outlines between man and woman, woman and man.

It's impossible to map this terrain, to explain why the clay gives in one spot and resists in another.

The Pipers merged their vast book collections, and any doubles (of Tennyson, Thoreau, James) were given away. She lost interest in classical music when jazz came along; they both adored June Christy and Fats Domino most of all. Henry began to cook and she sat back, enjoying his Swedish meatballs, garlic and lemon trout, and seeded breads. They invented a new language and embarrassing nicknames for each other, which they sometimes used in public:

spodie	caucus
pintel	gutcheon
hunca	munca

He finished her sentences. She supplied the word *putative* when it slipped his mind, if not at the moment then a few hours later. He so understood her need to leave a party early, he too became itchy and sullen at nine o'clock. They both sunk into a gloom during heavy rains, took turns reassuring the other: it's just the weather. Which became their explanation for any mood, dark or light: the miserable glorious weather. They tore a huge hole in a wall and filled it with glass, though it ruined the house lines and (a neighbor complained) opened their living room to the street.

In neriage, what is created from two distinct terrains is a fresh, negotiated *third* space. Each blended slab is unique: little landscapes of black hills and red canyons, red crests and black silhouettes, hot and cold rivers zigzagging side by side. A master handles the patterned slabs carefully, draping one into a mold as if nestling a newborn into a bassinet. Or wrapping another around a rolling pin to form a vase, stripes tumbling down like lava on volcanic rock.

A third space, cozy, warm, animal. Composed not exactly of shared palates, or preferences for Cubism. Not the one slate roof and nine-over-nine windows that sheltered the Pipers. Not jobs at the same university, not children. Not specific things, hers or his or theirs. Nor was it visible, this space, though they spent more and more of their time in it. A third space that expanded over the years, that seemed to travel wherever they went. More at home there than in their real home. More comfortable there than under their own skins.

"Can you give me the recipe for your beautiful glaze?" Such are the questions that plague Matsui Kosei, named Living National

Treasure for decades of work in nerikome, as neriage is sometimes called. No one knows the secrets to his particular technique, and no one will. "My colors are the colors of the future," he has been known to say.

What is the secret of a long marriage? Marianne and Henry's seventy-nine-year marriage came close to the longest in U.S. history (eighty-three years) and the world record (eighty-seven years), held by Karam and Kartari Chand from Bradford, United Kingdom.

They had more than six dozen children, grandchildren, and great-grandchildren. Their offspring composed one-third of the population of the town they settled in. More than seventy relatives attended their seventy-fifth-anniversary celebration, which was held in the very same rose garden they married in. It was later in May, and the Portlandias were in bloom. A gravel path surrounding the sundial was overwhelmed by thick, aromatic lilacs, and phlox bubbled over raised beds.

What cacophony, this mélange of Ellison noses and stubby fingers, Piper close-set eyes and long legs, black Piper tresses tied back with barrettes, strawberry Ellison crew cuts! Their Lutheran minister had long since died. His son settled the crowd with a sweep of his hand and launched into his homily.

"Clay lay in the earth millions of years," he began.

PER*f*ECT
Ending

Makes you want to begin, again.

NOTES AND SOURCES

~~~~

(On Lying)

The poem "Our Other Sister" originally appeared in Jeffrey Harrison's *Feeding the Fire* (Louisville, Ky.: Sarabande Books, 2001).

The poem "Homesickness" appears in Sarah Gorham's *Bad Daughter* (New York: Four Way Books, 2011).

(A Drinker's Guide to The Cat in the Hat*)*

The figure *Sources of Neurological Complications of Alcohol and Alcoholism* is from J. L. Bernat and M. Victor, "The Neurological Complications of Alcohol and Alcoholism." *Alcohol Health and Research World* 21, no. 1 (1997), 66.

Dr. Seuss, *The Cat in the Hat* (New York: Random House, 1957) and *The Cat in the Hat Comes Back* (New York: Random House, 1958).

Lindsey B. Zachary, "Formalist and Archetypal Interpretations of *The Cat in the Hat*." www.jbu.edu/assets/academics/journal/resource/file/2008.

(Sentimental à la Carte)

Figure *Mettigel* released into public domain by its author, *Stillife*, at the German Wikipedia project.

(The Shape of Fear)

Special thanks to Orlagh O'Brien and her website Emotionally} Vague, where I found the images for "The Shape of Fear": http://www.emotionallyvague.com/results_08.php.

(Be There No Human Here)

R. C. Lasiewski, *The Energetics of Migrating Hummingbirds*. Condor 64 (1962): 324.

Thanks to Laura Jensen for the borrowing from her poem "Window Views," which originally appeared in the collection *Shelter* (Port Townsend, Wash.: Dragon Gate Press, 1985).